Foreword

First and foremost, it's crucial to understand that this book is not financial advice. The content presented here serves as an introductory guide to how artificial intelligence tools might assist in personal finance and investment planning processes. All financial decisions should be made in consultation with qualified financial professionals who understand your specific circumstances, goals, and risk tolerance.

The landscape of artificial intelligence is evolving at an unprecedented pace. Each day brings new breakthroughs, tools, and capabilities that reshape our understanding of what's possible. This rapid evolution presents both exciting opportunities and important considerations for readers of this book.

While we have carefully selected and evaluated each tool and technology discussed in these pages, the nature of AI development means that by the time you read this, some tools may have evolved significantly, others may have been superseded by more advanced alternatives, and entirely new solutions may have emerged. This is not a limitation but rather a reflection of the dynamic and transformative nature of AI technology.

We encourage readers to approach this book as a foundation—a starting point for understanding the principles, possibilities, and practical applications of AI tools in personal finance. Before implementing any specific tool or solution discussed here, we strongly recommend:

> 1. Conducting current research to verify the tool's latest capabilities, limitations, and compatibility with your needs

> 2. Investigating newer alternatives that may have emerged since publication

3. Reviewing recent user experiences and professional evaluations

4. Considering the tool's ongoing development and support status

5. Assessing its integration with other current technologies in your stack

The core principles, strategies, and frameworks presented in this book remain valuable guides for evaluating and implementing AI solutions, even as specific tools evolve. We've focused on fundamental concepts that transcend individual products, enabling you to make informed decisions about current and future technologies.

Remember that the most effective AI implementation isn't necessarily about using the newest tool, but rather about choosing the right tool for your specific context, needs, and goals. Use this book as a compass to navigate the ever-expanding AI landscape, while staying alert to the constant evolution of the technology itself.

The journey into AI implementation is ongoing, and your success will depend on maintaining a balance between the timeless principles presented here and the dynamic nature of the technology itself. As you explore these tools, always remember that they are meant to supplement, not replace, sound financial judgment and professional advice.

. . .

For my girls, BTMM

The AI Investor: Smart Financial Planning in the Age of Artificial Intelligence

A beginner's guide to AI-Powered Personal Finance

Artificial Intelligence (AI) is no longer the stuff of science-fiction. It's right here, right now, and transforming industries at lightning speed. But let's be real—for most of us, AI can feel like a techy buzzword that's a bit intimidating. The good news? You don't need to be a coder or a Wall Street pro to harness AI for financial planning and investing. Whether you're 30, 70, or somewhere in between, this book will walk you through how to use AI tools to manage your money smarter, faster, and with a lot less stress.

This book is designed to be your comprehensive guide, expanding on every concept with real-world applications, actionable advice, and in-depth explanations. Each chapter begins with a detailed introduction, followed by practical tools, examples, and pro tips to help you confidently apply AI to your financial planning journey. By the time you finish, you'll not only understand AI but also know exactly how to use it to secure your financial future.

Why This Book Matters Now

The financial world is experiencing an unprecedented transformation. Traditional financial advice, once accessible only to the wealthy through expensive advisors, is now available to everyone through AI-powered tools. These tools are becoming increasingly sophisticated, offering personalized recommendations that were impossible just a few years ago. Whether you're trying to save for retirement, invest in the stock market, or simply budget better, AI tools can provide insights and guidance that were previously out of reach for the average person.

The AI Revolution in Personal Finance

The integration of AI into personal finance represents more than just technological advancement—it's a democratization of financial expertise. Consider these transformative changes:

- Automated investment platforms that once required millions in assets are now accessible with just a few hundred dollars
- Budgeting tools that learn from your spending patterns and provide personalized advice
- Risk assessment systems that continuously monitor your investments and adjust to market changes
- Tax optimization strategies that were once the domain of expensive accountants

Who This Book Is For

This guide is written for anyone who wants to take control of their financial future, regardless of their technical background or financial expertise. You might be:

- A young professional looking to start investing wisely
- A middle-aged parent planning for retirement and children's education
- A retiree seeking to optimize your investment strategy
- An entrepreneur managing irregular income

Remember, the goal isn't to replace human judgment with AI, but rather to enhance your decision-making capabilities with powerful technological tools. By the end of this book, you'll have the knowledge and confidence to use AI as a powerful ally in your financial journey.

Let's begin this exciting exploration of how AI can transform your approach to personal finance and help you achieve your financial goals more effectively than ever before.

Chapter 1:

What is AI, and Why Should You Care?

Now that you understand the transformative potential of AI in personal finance, let's dive deeper into what AI actually is and how it's revolutionizing financial management. The concepts we explore here will lay the foundation for the practical applications we'll discuss throughout this book.

Introduction to Artificial Intelligence

Artificial Intelligence (AI) has evolved from a sci-fi fantasy into a cornerstone of modern life, shaping industries, economies, and individual experiences. Its influence extends far beyond what we see on the surface, quietly integrating itself into everyday interactions and decision-making processes. From predicting what show you'll binge-watch next on Netflix to streamlining your daily commute with optimized routes on Google Maps, AI is everywhere. But let's zoom in on one question: How can this revolutionary technology help you better manage your money—and, by extension, your future?

At its core, AI is a simulation of human intelligence. It encompasses critical capabilities like problem-solving, decision-making, and learning from experiences. But unlike humans, AI doesn't need coffee breaks, doesn't get overwhelmed by too much data, and doesn't forget. Consider having a financial partner that works tirelessly to analyze millions of data points and suggests the best ways to save, invest, or spend, all tailored to your unique habits and goals. That's AI in action—a super-smart assistant built for the complexities of modern finance.

Common Misconceptions About AI in Finance

Before we dive deeper into AI's capabilities, let's address some common misconceptions that might be holding you back from embracing this powerful technology in your financial life.

Many people believe that AI financial tools require technical expertise to use effectively. "I'm not tech-savvy enough" is a common refrain among those hesitant to try AI-powered financial solutions. The reality is quite different. Modern AI financial tools are designed with user experience in mind, featuring intuitive interfaces that feel as familiar as your everyday banking app. If you can check your account balance or send money through your smartphone, you already have all the technical skills needed to leverage AI for your finances.

Another prevalent misconception is the idea that AI will eventually replace human financial advisors entirely. This fear stems from a misunderstanding of AI's role in financial services. Rather than replacing human expertise, AI serves as a powerful complement to traditional financial advice. Think of it as giving your financial advisor a supremely capable assistant who can process vast amounts of data and identify patterns in milliseconds. This collaboration between human insight and AI capabilities often leads to better outcomes than either could achieve alone. While AI handles data analysis and routine tasks, human advisors can focus on understanding your personal circumstances, emotional needs, and complex financial goals.

The notion that AI investment tools are inherently risky represents another significant misconception. Some worry that AI systems make financial decisions autonomously, without proper oversight or consideration of personal circumstances. In practice, AI investment tools typically implement conservative, well-researched strategies based on decades of financial theory and market data. These systems are often programmed to be more risk-aware than human investors, consistently applying tested investment principles rather than making emotional decisions during market volatility. They're designed to help you stay the course with your investment strategy, rather than chasing risky trends or making panic-driven decisions.

Security concerns also prevent many from embracing AI financial tools. The fear of entrusting sensitive financial data to AI systems is understandable in an era of frequent data breaches. However, reputable AI financial platforms typically employ security measures that match or exceed those of traditional banks. These systems use advanced encryption, multi-factor authentication, and continuous AI-powered security monitoring to protect your data. In fact, AI often adds an extra layer of security by detecting and preventing fraudulent activities more quickly and accurately than conventional security measures.

Cost represents another barrier for many potential users. There's a widespread belief that AI financial tools are expensive luxury services reserved for wealthy investors. This couldn't be further from the truth. The democratization of financial technology has made sophisticated AI tools accessible to everyone. Many platforms offer free basic services with premium features available for a modest fee. The cost savings from improved financial decisions and automated management often far exceed any subscription fees. Moreover, these tools can help you avoid costly financial mistakes and identify opportunities for savings that might otherwise go unnoticed.

How AI Actually Works in Personal Finance

Understanding how AI operates in the financial realm helps demystify its role in your financial journey. Unlike traditional financial software that follows rigid, pre-programmed rules, AI systems learn and adapt to your unique financial situation over time.

Pattern recognition represents one of AI's most powerful capabilities in personal finance. These systems analyze your transaction history with a level of detail and consistency impossible for humans to maintain. For example, an AI system might notice that you tend to overspend in the days following your paycheck deposit, or that your grocery bills spike during certain seasons. This detailed analysis goes beyond simple categorization, identifying subtle patterns that can inform better financial decisions. The system might suggest adjusting your automatic savings schedule or recommend bulk purchasing during sales periods to optimize your spending.

The continuous learning aspect of AI sets it apart from traditional financial tools. Your AI financial assistant constantly updates its understanding based on new information. If you change jobs and your income pattern shifts, the system adapts its recommendations accordingly. During market volatility, it might suggest portfolio adjustments based on your risk tolerance and investment timeline. This adaptive capability means your financial guidance evolves with your changing circumstances, rather than remaining static.

Personalization in AI financial tools goes far beyond basic customization options. These systems create truly individualized recommendations by synthesizing multiple data points about your financial life. They consider not just your income and expenses, but also your spending patterns, saving habits, investment preferences, and financial goals. This comprehensive analysis allows AI to provide nuanced recommendations that reflect your unique situation. For instance, rather than simply suggesting you cut back on dining out, an AI system might notice that you tend to eat out more during busy work periods and recommend meal preparation services or grocery delivery to help you maintain healthy eating habits while controlling costs.

To fully appreciate how AI achieved these sophisticated capabilities, it's helpful to understand its evolution over time. Let's explore the fascinating journey from AI's earliest concepts to its current role in revolutionizing personal finance.

A Brief History of AI and Personal Finance

To truly appreciate AI's current capabilities and future potential in personal finance, we need to understand how two parallel stories – the development of AI and the evolution of personal financial management – eventually converged to transform how we handle money.

1950s: The Birth of AI Research and Post-War Financial Growth

As Alan Turing proposed his groundbreaking ideas about machine intelligence in Britain, the global financial landscape was undergoing dramatic changes. While Turing worked on theoretical concepts that would later revolutionize computing, families worldwide were managing their money through decidedly analog means. In American households, the weekly pay envelope was king, with families carefully dividing cash into envelopes marked for different expenses – groceries, utilities, rent. In Japan, households meticulously maintained "kakeibo" ledgers, while British families often relied on the "tin box" method, separating coins and notes for different bills.

Banks in this era were transformation hubs, with rows of human "computers" – predominantly women – processing transactions by hand in massive ledger books. The introduction of the Diners Club card in 1950 marked a subtle but significant shift toward the future of electronic payments, though few could have predicted its eventual impact. Meanwhile, savings accounts came with physical passbooks, and Christmas Club accounts helped families budget for the holidays, with tellers hand-stamping deposit entries.

1960s-70s: Early AI Experiments Meet Financial Modernization

While scientists developed early AI programs to solve puzzles and play games, the banking world was experiencing its own technological revolution. The installation of the first ATM by Barclays Bank in London in 1967 marked a pivotal moment in banking convenience, though many customers were initially skeptical of these "robot tellers." In Japan, banks were pioneering the first online banking systems, while Swedish banks were early adopters of electronic payment processing.

The introduction of IBM's magnetic-strip cards began transforming banking operations, though the technology would take years to become ubiquitous. For most people, financial calculations meant using the revolutionary Bowmar 901B calculator or the HP-80, the first calculator specifically designed for financial calculations. These tools, while primitive by today's standards, represented a significant leap forward from manual calculations and paper ledgers.

1980s-90s: AI Winter and Digital Finance Revolution

The period known as the "AI Winter" coincided with a digital revolution in personal finance. While AI funding dried up in research labs, practical applications of technology in finance were flourishing. The launch of Quicken in 1983 transformed personal bookkeeping, while European consumers explored similar tools like Money Manager in the UK and Home Bank in France. The Bloomberg Terminal arrived in 1982, bringing real-time financial data to professional traders and eventually influencing how everyday investors would interact with financial information.

International banking underwent a fundamental shift with the expansion of the SWIFT network and the establishment of the Cirrus and Plus ATM networks, allowing travelers to access their money globally for the first time. In Japan, the creation of nationwide CD/ATM networks connected major banks, while European banking agreements began standardizing cross-border transactions. The introduction of Basel I Accords in 1988 created the first global banking standards, just as early neural networks were being tested for credit card fraud detection.

2000s-Present: The Convergence of AI and Personal Finance

The explosion of data and computing power ushered in an era where AI and personal finance finally merged. While Kenya pioneered mobile payments with M-PESA in 2007, China's Alipay was transforming digital transactions in Asia. Traditional banks faced competition from neobanks like Germany's N26 and Brazil's Nubank, which built their services around AI from the ground up.

The 2008 financial crisis catalyzed innovation in personal financial management tools, just as AI capabilities were maturing. Mint.com's 2006 launch revolutionized budget tracking, while robo-advisors emerged globally – *Betterment* in the US, *Nutmeg* in the UK, and *8 Securities* in Hong Kong. These platforms democratized sophisticated investment strategies previously available only to the wealthy.

Today, open banking initiatives worldwide have created a new financial ecosystem where AI can analyze data across multiple institutions, offering unprecedented insights into personal finances. From the biometric authentication on your banking app to the AI detecting fraudulent transactions in real-time, the technology that began with Turing's theoretical work has become an integral part of our financial lives. Whether you're using Sweden's Tink for personal finance management or

Japan's Money Forward for budgeting, AI is now your constant financial companion.

Looking ahead, the convergence of AI and finance continues to accelerate. The same systems that help Kenyan farmers receive payments through M-PESA can now predict market trends and optimize investment portfolios. The descendents of those early AI programs that played chess are now helping millions make smarter financial decisions every day, transcending borders and transforming how we think about money management.

How AI Works with Personal Finance: A Modern Perspective

In today's complex financial landscape, where the average person juggles multiple credit cards, subscription services, investment accounts, and digital payment platforms, managing money has become increasingly challenging. Consider your own financial life: you might start your day buying coffee with Apple Pay, check your investment app during lunch, receive a

Venmo request from a friend in the afternoon, and pay bills through your banking app in the evening. Each of these transactions generates data that, when properly analyzed, can reveal profound insights about your financial health.

The Power of AI in Modern Finance

Data Analysis at Lightning Speed

Remember the last time you visited a traditional financial advisor? They likely spent hours preparing for your meeting, manually reviewing your accounts and creating projections. Now imagine that same analysis happening continuously, 24/7, across all your financial activities. Modern AI systems process thousands of data points from your financial life in real-time – from your morning coffee purchase to your monthly Netflix subscription.

When you swipe your card at the grocery store, AI doesn't just record the transaction; it analyzes the purchase against your historical spending, current budget, and financial goals. It might notice that grocery prices in your area have increased 8% over the last three months and automatically adjust your budget categories. This kind of nuanced analysis, performed instantly across millions of transactions, was simply impossible in the pre-AI era.

Personalization in the Digital Age

The days of one-size-fits-all financial advice are over. Today's AI systems understand that your financial life is as unique as your fingerprint. Take the common challenge of managing irregular income – a reality for the growing gig economy workforce. Traditional budgeting methods often fall short for freelancers and contractors, but AI can adapt to these complex patterns.

For instance, when an AI system notices you're a freelancer with variable income, it might analyze your earnings patterns over the past year and create a dynamic savings strategy. During high-income months, it might automatically increase your savings rate, ensuring you have reserves for leaner periods. This level of personalization extends to investment strategies, debt repayment plans, and spending recommendations.

Automation for the Modern Consumer

In our fast-paced world, where the average person makes 150 financial decisions daily, automation isn't just convenient – it's essential for financial wellness. Modern AI tools function like a personal financial assistant, handling routine tasks while flagging important decisions for your attention.

Consider your investment portfolio. While you sleep, AI systems monitor global markets, adjusting your investments based on real-time events. If a major market shift occurs at 3 AM in Asian markets, your robo-advisor can rebalance your portfolio before you've had your morning coffee. The same automation applies to bill payments, subscription monitoring, and even negotiating bank fees.

Real-World Impact: Dr. Marcus Chen's Story

Dr. Marcus Chen's experience illustrates how AI transforms financial management for busy professionals. Like many millennials, Dr. Chen struggled to balance career demands with financial planning. His challenge wasn't just about saving money – it was about finding time to make informed financial decisions while working 60-hour weeks at his pediatric practice.

- Using modern AI tools, Dr. Chen created a seamless financial ecosystem:
- His morning coffee purchase automatically triggers a micro-investment in his portfolio
- An AI system monitors his student loan payments, adjusting his budget when interest rates change
- Smart alerts notify him about upcoming bills and potential savings opportunities
- His investment portfolio automatically rebalances based on his risk tolerance and market conditions

Within a year, this automated approach helped Dr. Chen increase his savings by 20% while reducing his financial management time to just 15 minutes per week. More importantly, he gained confidence in his financial decisions, knowing they were backed by continuous data analysis and personalized insights.

The Future of AI in Personal Finance

As we move forward, AI's role in personal finance continues to evolve. Emerging technologies are enabling even more sophisticated applications:

- Voice-activated financial assistants that can provide instant insights about your spending
- Predictive analytics that can forecast potential financial challenges months in advance
- Integration with smart home devices to optimize utility costs and household budgets
- Cross-platform analysis that provides a holistic view of your financial health across all accounts and investments

As we explore specific AI tools for budgeting and saving in the next chapter, you'll discover practical ways to implement these capabilities in your own financial life. From automated saving strategies to intelligent spending analysis, you'll learn how to leverage AI to transform your approach to money management.

Chapter 2:

AI Tools for Budgeting and Saving

Having explored the evolution of AI in finance, let's examine how modern AI tools are revolutionizing personal budgeting and saving. The sophisticated pattern recognition and predictive capabilities we discussed in Chapter 1 now power a new generation of financial management tools that make budgeting more accessible and effective than ever before.

Introduction to AI Budgeting Tools

Budgeting has traditionally been one of the most challenging aspects of personal finance. When income fluctuates or expenses spiral unexpectedly, even the most carefully planned budget can fall apart. AI budgeting tools address these age-old challenges by offering dynamic, data-driven solutions that adapt to your unique financial situation.

Unlike traditional methods that rely on manual tracking and static spreadsheets, AI brings a personalized, responsive approach to budgeting. These sophisticated systems learn from your spending patterns, anticipate future expenses, and provide actionable insights tailored to your specific habits and goals. The technology we explored in Chapter 1's history has evolved into practical tools that can transform how you manage money.

The Evolution of Budgeting Technology

The journey from basic spreadsheets to AI-powered financial platforms mirrors the broader evolution of personal computing and artificial intelligence. In the 1980s, the introduction of electronic spreadsheets marked the first significant shift away from paper-based budgeting. Programs like VisiCalc and later Excel revolutionized personal finance management, though they still required considerable manual effort. Users spent hours inputting every transaction, creating their own formulas, and maintaining complex workbooks. While this represented a step forward from paper ledgers, these tools were essentially digital versions of traditional accounting methods.

The 1990s ushered in dedicated personal finance software, marking a significant leap forward in functionality. Programs like Quicken and Microsoft Money introduced the ability to import bank transactions directly into your budget, eliminating much of the tedious data entry that characterized earlier tools. These applications offered predetermined categories for expenses and basic trend analysis, though their insights remained relatively simple. Users could, for the first time, generate reports and charts to visualize their spending patterns, but the software couldn't provide predictive insights or personalized recommendations. The major limitation was their desktop-based nature – your financial information remained trapped on a single computer.

The dawn of the internet age in the 2000s transformed budgeting technology once again. Online banking tools and web-based platforms like Mint emerged, offering real-time access to financial information from anywhere. These services introduced automated transaction categorization, though early attempts were often imprecise and required frequent manual corrections. The ability to view transactions as they occurred, rather than waiting to import them manually, gave users unprecedented visibility into their spending. However, these tools still relied on rigid rules and predetermined categories, lacking the adaptability to learn from individual user behaviors.

Today's AI-powered financial platforms represent a quantum leap in capability and sophistication. Modern budgeting tools employ advanced pattern recognition algorithms that learn from millions of transactions across their user base while maintaining privacy and security. They can not only categorize spending with remarkable accuracy but also predict future expenses based on historical patterns and emerging trends. These systems understand context – they can differentiate between a grocery purchase at Walmart and an electronics purchase at the same store, something that stumped earlier tools.

The integration of behavioral science with artificial intelligence has enabled these platforms to provide truly personalized guidance. Rather than simply tracking spending, modern AI tools can identify potential savings opportunities, predict cash flow issues before they occur, and suggest specific actions based on your unique financial situation. Cross-platform integration means your financial information syncs seamlessly across devices, while machine learning algorithms continuously improve their understanding of your habits and preferences.

Looking ahead, the next evolution in budgeting technology is already taking shape. Emerging AI systems are beginning to incorporate external data sources – from local economic indicators to global market trends – to provide even more sophisticated financial guidance. The future promises tools that can not only track and predict but actively negotiate better rates for your bills, identify optimal timing for major purchases, and provide increasingly sophisticated investment advice based on your personal goals and risk tolerance.

Modern AI Capabilities in Budgeting

Today's AI budgeting tools leverage several sophisticated technologies:

Natural Language Processing (NLP)
Modern AI platforms can understand and categorize transactions by interpreting merchant names, descriptions, and even your personal labels. For instance, when you buy coffee from "Joe's Corner Café," the system recognizes this as a dining expense rather than groceries, learning from both the merchant name and your spending patterns.

Predictive Analytics
Using historical data and machine learning algorithms, these tools can forecast your future expenses with remarkable accuracy. They analyze seasonal patterns, recurring bills, and spending habits to help you prepare for upcoming costs before they arise.

Behavioral Analysis
AI systems study your unique financial behaviors to provide personalized guidance. Rather than applying

one-size-fits-all rules, they learn your specific patterns and preferences, adapting their recommendations accordingly.

Case Study: AI-Powered Savings Success

Consider the experience of Jasmine Chen, a freelance web developer with variable monthly income. Unlike the traditional "save 20% of your income" advice that didn't work for her irregular earnings, AI-powered budgeting tools transformed her approach to saving:

First Month:

- The AI analyzed her income patterns over six months
- Identified "safe to save" amounts during peak earning periods

- Created a flexible saving schedule aligned with her project payment dates

After Six Months:

- Accumulated $3,000 in emergency savings

- Reduced unnecessary subscription costs by 40%
- Established a sustainable saving pattern despite income variability

Conclusion: The Future of AI-Powered Financial Management

As we've explored throughout this chapter, AI has transformed budgeting and saving from tedious manual tasks into an intelligent, automated process that adapts to your unique financial life. From the early days of electronic spreadsheets to today's sophisticated AI platforms, the evolution of financial technology has democratized access to powerful money management tools that were once available only to financial professionals.

Personalization is Key

The most significant advantage of AI-powered budgeting tools is their ability to learn from your specific financial patterns and behaviors. Unlike traditional budgeting methods that apply one-size-fits-all rules, these systems adapt to your unique situation, whether you're dealing with irregular income, variable expenses, or complex financial goals.

Tools for Every Style

From hands-on budget managers to those who prefer a more automated approach, AI tools have evolved to accommodate different preferences and needs. The variety of available platforms ensures that everyone can find a solution that matches their preferred level of engagement and financial management style.

Looking Ahead

As AI technology continues to advance, we can expect even more sophisticated features that will further simplify financial management while providing deeper insights. The integration of augmented reality, predictive life event planning, and comprehensive financial ecosystems promises to make money management increasingly intuitive and effective.

While effective budgeting and saving form the foundation of financial health, growing your wealth often requires taking the next step into investing. In Chapter 3, we'll explore how AI is revolutionizing the investment landscape, making sophisticated investment strategies accessible to everyone, regardless of their experience or account size. You'll discover how the same AI capabilities that power your budgeting tools are being applied to help you make smarter investment decisions and build long-term wealth.

Chapter 3:
Investing Basics for Beginners - The AI Revolution

The world of investing has long been shrouded in mystique, often feeling like a private club with its own impenetrable language and unwritten rules. For decades, successful investing seemed to require either deep expertise or the means to hire expensive financial advisors. The typical person's introduction to investing often came through a workplace 401(k), accompanied by a bewildering array of fund choices and little guidance beyond a basic risk questionnaire.

But today's investment landscape is undergoing a profound transformation. Artificial intelligence has emerged as a great democratizer, breaking down the traditional barriers that kept many people from participating in the markets. This transformation couldn't be more timely – in an era of rising inflation and increasing life expectancy, the old advice of "just save your money" no longer suffices for building long-term financial security.

Consider the reality facing most people today: bank savings accounts offer interest rates that barely register above zero, while inflation steadily erodes purchasing power. A dollar saved in 2010 is worth significantly less today, yet many people still keep substantial portions of their wealth in low-yield savings accounts out of fear or uncertainty about investing. This hesitation is understandable – the investment world can seem overwhelming with its array of stocks, bonds, ETFs, mutual funds, and cryptocurrencies, each carrying its own complex set of risks and potential rewards.

This is where AI enters the picture, transforming the investment process from an intimidating maze into an accessible path forward. Modern AI-powered investment platforms don't just simplify the process; they fundamentally reshape how individuals can approach growing their wealth. These systems analyze millions of data points across global markets, economic indicators, and individual financial situations to create personalized investment strategies that once required teams of human analysts to develop.

Understanding Investment Fundamentals in the AI Era

Before diving deeper into AI-powered investing, it's essential to understand the basic building blocks that these sophisticated systems work with. Think of these fundamentals as the language AI uses to construct your financial future.

Core Investment Vehicles

Modern investment portfolios typically consist of several key components, each serving a specific purpose in your financial strategy. AI systems are particularly adept at balancing these elements based on your goals:

Stocks: Ownership in Innovation

When you own stocks, you're buying a piece of a company's future. While individual stock picking can be risky, AI platforms typically invest in broad collections of stocks through ETFs and mutual funds. For instance, when Betterment's AI suggests a stock allocation, it's not betting on individual companies like Apple or Tesla, but rather providing exposure to entire markets or sectors.

Bonds: The Stability Foundation

Bonds represent loans to governments or corporations, providing regular interest payments and generally lower risk than stocks. AI systems dynamically adjust your bond allocation based on multiple factors – not just your age (as in traditional advice) but also your income stability, risk tolerance, and market conditions.

ETFs (Exchange-Traded Funds): The Modern Portfolio Builder

ETFs have become the preferred tool of AI investment platforms because they offer instant diversification at low cost. When Wealthfront's AI constructs a portfolio, it might use an ETF that tracks the entire U.S. stock market (providing exposure to thousands of companies) rather than trying to pick individual winners.

Understanding Risk and Return

AI has revolutionized how we think about the risk-return relationship. Traditional advisors might simply ask about your risk tolerance on a scale of 1-10, but AI platforms take a more nuanced approach:

Risk Assessment in Practice

Consider how M1 Finance's AI evaluates risk tolerance. Instead of just asking how you feel about market drops, it analyzes:

- Your actual behavior during market volatility
- Your financial commitments and timeline
- Your income stability and emergency savings
- Your past investment experiences
- Your specific financial goals and their urgency

The Power of Diversification

AI systems excel at creating truly diversified portfolios that go beyond simple stock-bond splits. They might include:

- Geographic diversification across global markets
- Sector diversification to reduce industry-specific risks
- Asset class diversification including real estate investment trusts (REITs) and treasury inflation-protected securities (TIPS)
- Factor diversification considering value, growth, and momentum strategies

Time Horizons and Investment Goals

AI platforms have transformed how we match investments to specific life goals. Rather than treating all your money as one pool, these systems can create distinct investment strategies for different objectives:

Short-Term Goals (0-3 years)

For near-term objectives like saving for a home down payment, AI might recommend:

- Higher allocation to stable, liquid investments
- Smart cash management tools that maximize interest while maintaining safety
- Dynamic rebalancing to protect accumulated gains

Medium-Term Goals (3-10 years)

For goals like saving for a child's education, AI systems typically suggest:

- Balanced portfolios with moderate growth potential
- Automated risk reduction as the goal date approaches
- Tax-optimized investment strategies

Long-Term Goals (10+ years)

For retirement and other long-term objectives, AI platforms often recommend:

- Higher allocation to growth investments
- More aggressive tax-loss harvesting
- Sophisticated rebalancing strategies

The Role of Fees and Taxes

One of AI's most significant contributions to investing is its ability to minimize the impact of fees and taxes, which can significantly erode returns over time. Modern platforms optimize for:

Fee Efficiency

- Using low-cost ETFs instead of expensive actively managed funds
- Minimizing transaction costs through smart rebalancing
- Reducing advisory fees through automation

Tax Intelligence

- Automated tax-loss harvesting to offset gains
- Strategic dividend reinvestment
- Tax-aware rebalancing that minimizes taxable events

With these fundamental concepts in mind, let's explore how AI tools apply these principles to create and manage sophisticated investment strategies tailored to your specific situation.

The sophistication of today's AI investment tools extends far beyond basic portfolio management. These systems can:

- Analyze your entire financial picture, including debt, savings, and future financial commitments
- Assess your true risk tolerance through behavioral analysis rather than just questionnaires
- Monitor global market conditions 24/7 and adjust strategies in real-time
- Optimize tax efficiency through automated loss harvesting and strategic rebalancing
- Provide contextualized education about investment concepts as you encounter them

Leading platforms in this space have developed distinct approaches to AI-powered investing:

Betterment: Pioneered automated portfolio management with a focus on long-term passive investing

Wealthfront: Emphasizes tax-optimization and advanced financial planning features

Ellevest: Addresses specific challenges in women's financial planning and investing

SoFi Automated Investing: Combines robo-advisory services with access to human financial planners

M1 Finance: Offers customizable automated investing with flexible portfolio options

Vanguard Digital Advisor: Brings the low-cost index fund pioneer's philosophy to automated investing

The impact of these platforms extends beyond just making investing more accessible. They're fundamentally changing how people think about and interact with their investments. Instead of anxiously watching stock tickers or making emotional decisions during market volatility, investors can now rely on AI systems that maintain strategic discipline regardless of market conditions.

Take the experience of Dr. Sarah Park, a 45-year-old high school chemistry teacher who had always found investing intimidating. Like many educators, she had access to a 403(b) retirement plan but struggled to make informed decisions about her investments. After years of leaving her retirement savings in an ultra-conservative money market fund, she decided to try a robo-advisor platform. The AI system analyzed her complete financial picture – including her pension projections, risk tolerance, and retirement timeline – to create a diversified portfolio strategy.

The system didn't just select investments; it educated Dr. Park along the way, explaining concepts like asset allocation and market volatility in clear, contextual ways. When markets experienced turbulence, the platform provided calm, data-driven perspectives that helped her maintain her long-term strategy instead of making emotional decisions. Over her first year using the platform, her portfolio grew by 8%, but more importantly, she gained confidence in her financial future.

This transformation of investing from an elite pursuit into an accessible tool for wealth building represents one of AI's most significant contributions to personal finance. Whether you're starting with $100 or $100,000, whether you're a market novice or an experienced investor, AI tools can help you develop and maintain an investment strategy aligned with your goals.

As we explore deeper into AI-powered investing in this chapter, you'll discover how these tools can help you:

- Develop a personalized investment strategy based on your unique situation
- Understand and manage investment risk effectively
- Navigate market volatility with confidence
- Build long-term wealth while minimizing fees and taxes
- Make informed decisions about your financial future

The Technology Behind AI-Powered Investing

How Robo-Advisors Think and Learn

Modern robo-advisors represent a fascinating convergence of financial theory and artificial intelligence. Consider how Wealthfront's AI system approaches portfolio construction: it doesn't simply assign you to a pre-built portfolio based on age and risk tolerance. Instead, it analyzes over 400,000 data points about your financial life – from spending patterns to investment preferences – to create a truly personalized strategy. When you make a large purchase or receive a bonus, the system automatically recalibrates its understanding of your financial situation and adjusts its investment approach accordingly.

Take the case of Marcus Rodriguez, a freelance software developer whose income fluctuates seasonally. Traditional investment advice about "investing 20% of your monthly income" wasn't practical for his situation. Wealthfront's AI analyzed two years of his income patterns and created a dynamic investment strategy that automatically increased investments during his high-earning months and reduced them during slower periods. The system even anticipated his quarterly tax payments and adjusted investment schedules around them.

The Science of Risk Assessment

Modern AI platforms have revolutionized how we measure and manage investment risk. Betterment, for instance, uses a sophisticated form of risk analysis called "downside risk modeling." Instead of just asking how you feel about market volatility, their AI monitors your behavior during market downturns. Do you log in more frequently when markets are volatile? Do you tend to sell when markets drop? The system uses these behavioral insights to adjust your risk profile and investment mix dynamically.

For example, when global markets tumbled in early 2020, Betterment's AI noted that users who received proactive explanations about market volatility were 60% less likely to make panic-driven investment changes. This led to the development of "smart notifications" – AI-triggered communications that provide context and reassurance during market turbulence, essentially acting as a behavioral coach.

Democratizing Sophisticated Investment Strategies

Today's AI investment tools are bringing formerly exclusive investment strategies to everyday investors. Consider these real-world applications:

Tax-Loss Harvesting
Wealthfront's automated tax-loss harvesting algorithm continuously monitors your portfolio for opportunities to capture tax benefits. When the 2020 market decline occurred, their system automatically harvested losses for clients, generating tax savings that averaged 5.8

times the annual advisory fee for portfolios over
$100,000.

Factor Investing

Dimensional Fund Advisors, traditionally only available
through select financial advisors, now offers AI-driven
factor investing through platforms like Betterment. This
sophisticated strategy, which targets specific drivers of
returns like value and momentum, is now accessible to
investors starting with just $10.

ESG (Environmental, Social, and Governance)
Integration

Ellevest's AI system can now analyze thousands of
companies for ESG compliance while maintaining
optimal portfolio performance. When a client expresses
interest in sustainable investing, the system
automatically identifies replacements for non-compliant
investments without sacrificing returns.

The Psychology of AI-Assisted Investing

Understanding human behavior is crucial for successful
investing, and AI platforms have become remarkably

adept at managing the psychological aspects of investing. M1 Finance, for example, has developed what they call "Emotional Intelligence Protocols" – AI systems that recognize and respond to patterns of emotional investing.

Consider these behavioural finance features:

Pattern Recognition and Intervention
When the system detects that you're likely to make an emotion-driven investment decision (like selling during a market dip), it intervenes with:
- Historical data showing similar market situations and their outcomes
- Personalized reminders of your long-term goals
- Alternative actions that align with your investment strategy

Goal Visualization
SoFi's AI creates dynamic visualizations that show how today's investment decisions impact your future goals. When you consider reducing your investment contributions, the system instantly shows the

compound effect on your retirement date or other financial goals.

Real-Time Market Analysis and Response

Modern AI investment platforms process market data at unprecedented speeds and scales. Here's how they're transforming market analysis:

News Sentiment Analysis

Wealthfront's systems analyze over 1,000 news sources every minute, evaluating how global events might impact different asset classes. During major events like Brexit or the COVID-19 pandemic, this allowed their portfolios to adjust more quickly than traditional managed funds.

Market Correlation Detection

Betterment's AI continuously monitors correlations between different asset classes, automatically adjusting portfolios when traditional relationships between stocks and bonds shift. This became particularly valuable during the unusual market conditions of 2020-2021.

As we explore these technological capabilities, it's important to understand how to choose the right AI investment platform for your needs. In the next section, we'll examine specific criteria for evaluating different platforms and how to match their features with your investment goals.

Chapter 4:

AI for Risk Management

The Evolution of Risk Management in the AI Era

Risk management is the strategic process of identifying, assessing, and mitigating potential threats to financial investments. At its core, it's about understanding and balancing potential rewards against potential losses. Every investment carries inherent risks—from market volatility and economic shifts to industry-specific challenges and global events. Traditionally, investors have sought to protect their portfolios by diversifying investments, setting stop-loss orders, and carefully analyzing market trends.

However, the landscape of risk management has been dramatically transformed by artificial intelligence. In the past, investors relied on gut feelings, experience, and simple rules of thumb to navigate financial uncertainties. A seasoned financial advisor might have spent hours manually analyzing company reports and market trends, using intuition to manage potential risks.

Today, AI has revolutionized risk management, turning it from an art into a precise, data-driven science. Modern AI tools excel at providing clear, comprehensive insights by analyzing vast amounts of data that would be impossible for human analysts to process manually. These tools combine advanced data science and machine learning to predict market movements with remarkable accuracy, examining everything from economic indicators and company performance metrics to global events and emerging trends.

The power of AI in risk management lies in its ability to recognize complex patterns and correlations that might escape human perception. By scanning countless data points—including financial markets, global weather patterns, geopolitical events, and even social media sentiment—AI provides a holistic view of potential risks and opportunities. For instance, an AI system might detect early signs of a political crisis in a major economy, flag an upcoming storm season that could impact crop yields, or identify subtle market volatility before significant losses occur.

What makes this technological evolution particularly transformative is how it has democratized sophisticated risk management. Strategies once exclusively available to hedge funds and institutional investors are now accessible to individual investors through user-friendly apps and platforms. A veteran financial advisor who witnessed this transformation can now use AI tools that process complex information in seconds, providing insights far beyond what was possible in previous decades.

By combining predictive analytics, pattern recognition, and real-time global data analysis, AI has transformed risk management from a reactive practice into a proactive science. Investors of all levels can now anticipate market shifts, strategically position their portfolios, and make more informed decisions—turning what was once an uncertain art into a precise, data-driven approach to protecting and growing investments.

How AI Evaluates Risk

AI-powered tools are like having a crystal ball—but one based on hard data and algorithms. These sophisticated systems analyze historical market performance to identify trends, such as how certain asset classes react to economic shifts or crises. They use complex algorithms to predict the likelihood of future market fluctuations, taking into account countless variables humans might miss. For instance, they can flag sectors vulnerable to downturns before signs become obvious to the average investor.

Perhaps most importantly, AI helps investors spread their investments across different asset classes—like stocks, bonds, real estate, and even alternative investments like commodities or cryptocurrencies—to minimize risk while maximizing returns. This isn't just about following the old adage of not putting all your eggs in one basket; it's about using data-driven insights to determine exactly how many eggs should go in each basket for optimal results.

Understanding Risk Types Through AI's Lens

Modern AI systems have revolutionized our understanding of investment risk by revealing its multifaceted nature. While traditional investors might have focused primarily on market risk—the possibility of losing money due to general market movements—AI has illuminated a complex web of interconnected risks. For instance, when analyzing a seemingly straightforward investment in a U.S. technology company, AI might identify exposure to semiconductor supply chains in Asia, regulatory changes in Europe, and even climate-related risks affecting data center operations.

This deeper understanding becomes particularly valuable when examining how different types of risk interact. Take the case of a regional bank stock that appears stable based on traditional metrics. AI analysis might reveal hidden risks by connecting dots between local real estate trends, changes in employment patterns, and shifts in demographic data. These insights help investors understand not just what risks exist, but how they might compound or offset each other in different scenarios.

The real power of AI in risk analysis lies in its ability to quantify and compare different types of risk across various time horizons. For instance, while currency risk might pose an immediate threat to international investments, technological disruption might represent a longer-term risk to established industries. AI helps investors balance these varying risk factors and time horizons, creating more resilient portfolios that can weather different types of market stress.

Real-World Example: Reducing Portfolio Volatility

Let's bring this to life with a practical example. Meet Sarah, a new investor who wanted to build a balanced portfolio. Initially, Sarah's investments leaned heavily toward high-risk tech stocks. She used an AI-powered tool like Personal Capital to analyze her portfolio. The results were eye-opening—her concentration in tech stocks had created a level of risk she hadn't realized she was taking.

The AI flagged her portfolio's high volatility and suggested diversification strategies. By reallocating 20% of her funds into government bonds and 15% into real estate investment trusts (REITs), Sarah reduced her portfolio's risk while maintaining growth potential. Over the next year, her portfolio weathered a market dip far better than if she'd stuck to her original allocation. This real-world example demonstrates how AI can help investors make more informed decisions about risk management.

AI Beyond Numbers: Managing Emotional Risk

Investing isn't just a numbers game; it's also a mental one. Emotional decisions can lead to unnecessary risk—like panic-selling during a market dip. This is where AI truly shines, acting as an objective advisor that isn't swayed by fear or greed. When markets become volatile, AI tools send automated alerts about changes in your portfolio or market conditions, helping you act calmly and strategically rather than emotionally.

Some platforms go even further, analyzing your investment behavior to identify patterns. For example, if you tend to sell off investments too early, missing out on potential gains, the AI might suggest sticking to your strategy for longer periods. This behavioral coaching aspect of AI helps investors overcome their own psychological biases—often the biggest risk to long-term investment success.

AI's Early Warning System

The predictive capabilities of AI have transformed how investors receive and react to warning signs in the market. Unlike human analysts who might need to see multiple clear signals before identifying a trend, AI can detect subtle changes across thousands of data points that might indicate upcoming market shifts. During the early stages of major market events, AI systems have often provided crucial early warnings by identifying unusual patterns in trading volumes, changes in institutional investor behavior, or shifts in market sentiment.

These early warning capabilities extend far beyond traditional market indicators. Modern AI systems constantly analyze satellite imagery, social media trends, patent filings, and countless other data sources to identify potential risks and opportunities. For example, one AI system detected early signs of supply chain disruptions in 2021 by analyzing shipping container movements and port activity levels months before these issues became widely reported. This allowed proactive investors to adjust their portfolios and hedge against potential impacts.

The sophistication of these warning systems continues to evolve. Machine learning algorithms now understand context and nuance in ways that were impossible just a few years ago. They can distinguish between temporary market noise and significant shifts, helping investors avoid both overreaction to minor fluctuations and underreaction to major changes. This balanced approach to risk detection helps investors stay ahead of market movements while avoiding the costly mistakes that come from false alarms.

The Human-AI Partnership in Risk Management

The most successful approach to risk management isn't about choosing between human judgment and artificial intelligence—it's about creating an effective partnership between the two. Think of AI as an incredibly knowledgeable research assistant who can process vast amounts of information but relies on human wisdom for context and final decisions. This partnership becomes particularly powerful when dealing with unprecedented situations where historical data alone may not provide all the answers.

Consider the experience of Maria, a retired teacher who uses AI tools to manage her retirement portfolio. While the AI provides detailed analysis and suggestions, Maria's understanding of her own risk tolerance and life circumstances informs how she applies these recommendations. During market volatility, she uses AI insights to understand market conditions but combines this with her personal knowledge about upcoming expenses and peace of mind requirements to make final decisions.

The key to successful human-AI partnership lies in understanding the strengths and limitations of each. AI excels at processing data, identifying patterns, and maintaining emotional neutrality, while humans bring contextual understanding, judgment in unusual situations, and the ability to consider personal circumstances that might not be captured in data. Learning to balance these complementary capabilities can lead to better risk management outcomes than either humans or AI could achieve alone.

Customizing Risk Management

The true power of AI in risk management lies in its ability to adapt strategies to individual circumstances. Unlike traditional one-size-fits-all approaches, AI can consider a person's complete financial picture—including factors like job stability, industry sector, geographic location, and family obligations—to create truly personalized risk management strategies. For instance, an AI system might recommend different risk management approaches for two investors of the same age and wealth level if one works in a stable government job while the other runs a seasonal business.

This personalization becomes particularly valuable when dealing with unique situations that don't fit traditional models. Take the case of David, a freelance consultant with irregular income patterns. Traditional risk management approaches struggled to accommodate his variable cash flow, but AI tools helped create a flexible strategy that adjusted risk levels based on his income cycles. During high-income periods, the system automatically increased his investment in stable assets, building a buffer for leaner times.

The customization extends beyond just financial factors to include behavioral and emotional considerations. AI systems learn from how individuals react to market movements and adjust their recommendations accordingly. For someone who tends to make emotional investment decisions during market volatility, the system might suggest more conservative allocations or implement automatic rebalancing to prevent impulsive changes. This deep level of personalization helps ensure that risk management strategies are not just technically sound but also practically implementable for each individual.

Risk Management in Practice

The daily practice of risk management with AI looks very different from traditional approaches. Instead of periodic portfolio reviews or annual rebalancing, modern AI-driven risk management is a continuous, dynamic process. Each morning might bring new insights about market conditions, potential risks, or opportunities for portfolio optimization. The key is establishing a routine that makes effective use of these tools without becoming overwhelmed by information.

Take the example of Robert, a small business owner who carved out 15 minutes each morning to review his AI-generated risk reports. He set up custom alerts for specific conditions—like significant changes in sector concentrations or unusual market movements—but relied on the AI to filter out noise and highlight only meaningful developments. This systematic approach helped him stay informed without letting investment management consume his day.

The practical implementation of AI risk management also involves setting up appropriate boundaries and automation rules. While AI can provide 24/7 monitoring and analysis, successful investors learn to establish clear guidelines for when and how they'll respond to different types of alerts. This might mean automatically rebalancing when portfolios drift beyond certain thresholds, but requiring human review for more significant changes. Creating these structured processes helps investors maintain discipline while making the most of AI capabilities.

Learning from Market Stress

Market stress periods provide valuable lessons about the effectiveness of AI-driven risk management strategies. During the 2020 market downturn, AI systems demonstrated their value not just in identifying risks but in helping investors maintain perspective. While many investors made emotional decisions to sell at market lows, those using AI tools often received contextual analysis that helped them stick to their long-term strategies.

These stress periods also reveal how AI systems learn and adapt. Each market crisis presents unique challenges, but AI's ability to analyze historical patterns while adapting to new situations proves invaluable. For instance, during recent inflation concerns, AI systems helped investors understand how different assets might perform by analyzing historical inflation periods while accounting for modern market structures and policy responses.

The lessons learned during market stress help improve future risk management capabilities. AI systems now incorporate insights from past crises to better identify warning signs and suggest protective measures. This continuous learning process helps investors prepare for future challenges while avoiding the mistakes of the past. The key is understanding that market stress is inevitable, but proper preparation can help minimize its impact on investment portfolios.

The Future of AI Risk Management

The frontier of AI risk management continues to expand with new technologies and capabilities. Emerging trends include the use of quantum computing to model complex risk scenarios, natural language processing to analyze company earnings calls for subtle warning signs, and advanced visualization tools that make risk insights more intuitive and actionable. These developments promise to make risk management even more sophisticated while remaining accessible to average investors.

Perhaps most exciting is the development of AI systems that can anticipate and adapt to structural changes in markets. Traditional risk models often struggle when market dynamics shift, but new AI approaches are better at identifying emerging trends and adjusting strategies accordingly. For instance, some systems are already incorporating analysis of cryptocurrency markets, climate risk, and changing demographic patterns to help investors prepare for future challenges.

As these technologies evolve, the focus remains on making sophisticated risk management more accessible and effective for individual investors. The future likely holds more personalized risk management solutions, better integration of various data sources, and more intuitive ways to understand and act on risk insights. For investors, the key is staying informed about these developments while maintaining a balanced perspective on how to best use these tools in their own investment journey.

Conclusion

Risk management isn't about avoiding risk altogether; it's about understanding and balancing it. AI makes this process more accessible, less overwhelming, and— dare we say—even enjoyable. By leveraging these tools, you can make informed decisions, avoid emotional pitfalls, and build a portfolio that aligns with your financial goals.

That said, it's crucial to remember that this book is not intended to provide financial advice. The tools and techniques discussed here are meant to educate and empower you to take control of your financial journey. Any actions you take should be carefully considered and supported by additional research and, if necessary, consultation with financial professionals. Investing always carries inherent risks, and while AI can help you manage them, there are no guarantees.

Ultimately, the goal is to equip you with the knowledge and confidence to navigate the complexities of investing. Whether you're using AI tools to diversify your portfolio, mitigate risk, or keep your emotions in check, always approach investing with a mindset of learning, adaptability, and due diligence. The future of finance is here, and with AI as your ally, you're better prepared to seize it responsibly.

Chapter 5:

AI for Retirement Planning

The Evolution of Retirement Planning

The landscape of retirement planning has transformed dramatically over the past decades. Gone are the days when workers could rely solely on company pensions and Social Security. Today's retirement reality demands a more sophisticated approach, one where artificial intelligence plays an increasingly crucial role in navigating complex decisions and market uncertainties.

The Modern Retirement Challenge

Traditional retirement planning methods suffered from significant limitations that made it difficult for individuals to create truly effective long-term strategies. Static calculations failed to adapt to changing market conditions, leaving retirement plans vulnerable to unexpected shifts in the economic landscape. The prevalent one-size-fits-all approaches ignored crucial individual circumstances that could dramatically impact retirement outcomes. These traditional methods also struggled with processing multiple scenarios simultaneously, making it challenging to evaluate different retirement paths effectively. Perhaps most concerning was their insufficient consideration of longevity risk and healthcare costs, two factors that have become increasingly important in modern retirement planning. The reliance on manual updates often led to outdated projections that failed to reflect current market conditions or personal circumstances.

AI has revolutionized these aspects by providing dynamic, personalized solutions that evolve with changing circumstances and market conditions. These sophisticated systems can process vast amounts of data in real-time, offering insights and adjustments that would be impossible with traditional planning methods.

How AI Transforms Retirement Planning

Real-Time Analysis and Adaptation

Modern AI retirement tools have introduced a level of sophistication and responsiveness previously unimaginable in retirement planning. These systems continuously monitor market performance and economic indicators, providing immediate adjustments to retirement strategies when conditions change. They track changes in personal income and spending patterns, ensuring that retirement projections remain accurate and achievable. When retirement goals or risk tolerance shift, the AI adapts instantly, recalibrating investment strategies and savings recommendations accordingly.

Healthcare cost projections, a critical component of retirement planning, receive constant updates based on the latest data and trends. Social Security optimization opportunities are continuously evaluated, ensuring that retirees maximize their benefits based on their unique circumstances. When tax laws change, these systems immediately assess the impact on retirement accounts and adjust strategies to maintain optimal tax efficiency.

Case Study: The Thompson Family's Retirement Journey

Sarah and Michael Thompson's experience illustrates the transformative power of AI in retirement planning. At age 45, this professional couple thought they had their retirement well in hand with $400,000 in their 401(k) accounts and monthly savings of $1,500. They had set their sights on retiring at 65, feeling confident in their progress toward this goal.

However, when they began using an AI-powered retirement planning system, they discovered several critical blind spots in their strategy. The AI analysis revealed they had significantly underestimated their healthcare costs, projecting a shortfall of $300,000 in their medical expense planning. Their investment allocation, while seemingly prudent, was actually too conservative for their twenty-year timeline to retirement, potentially leaving significant growth opportunity on the table. The system also identified that their planned Social Security claiming strategy was suboptimal, potentially costing them thousands in lifetime benefits. Furthermore, they were missing several opportunities for tax efficiency in their retirement savings approach.

Armed with these insights, the Thompsons worked with their AI planning tool to implement a revised strategy. They increased their monthly savings to $2,000 after the system helped them identify areas in their budget where they could redirect funds to retirement savings. Their investment allocation was adjusted to better align with their time horizon and risk tolerance, creating greater potential for long-term growth. They developed a more comprehensive healthcare savings strategy and optimized their planned Social Security claiming approach. These changes, working in concert, eliminated their projected retirement shortfall and put them on track for a more secure retirement.

Advanced Features of AI Retirement Tools

Dynamic Withdrawal Strategies

The conventional wisdom of retirement withdrawals has been dominated by simple rules of thumb, such as the famous 4% withdrawal rule. However, AI platforms have revolutionized this aspect of retirement planning by introducing sophisticated, adaptive approaches that respond to real-world conditions. These systems continuously monitor market performance, personal circumstances, and economic indicators to adjust withdrawal recommendations in real-time.

Modern AI platforms consider multiple factors when determining optimal withdrawal strategies. They analyze market conditions to recommend when to increase or decrease withdrawals, helping retirees preserve their nest egg during market downturns while taking advantage of strong performance periods. Tax optimization plays a crucial role in these calculations, with AI systems orchestrating withdrawals across different account types—traditional IRAs, Roth accounts, and taxable investments—to minimize the tax burden each year.

The management of Required Minimum Distributions (RMDs) has become particularly sophisticated under AI guidance. These systems look ahead to project RMD requirements and plan withdrawals years in advance, helping retirees avoid tax surprises and maintain a stable income stream. They coordinate these withdrawals with Social Security benefits, creating a comprehensive income strategy that maximizes after-tax income while maintaining financial security.

Intelligent Portfolio Management

AI has transformed portfolio management in retirement from a periodic rebalancing exercise into a dynamic, continuous optimization process. These systems monitor portfolios around the clock, making subtle adjustments as market conditions change and retirement needs evolve. The asset allocation process has become increasingly sophisticated, with AI tools considering not just age and risk tolerance, but also factors like health status, family longevity, and specific retirement lifestyle goals.

Tax-loss harvesting, once a year-end consideration, now occurs automatically throughout the year as opportunities arise. These systems can identify and execute tax-loss harvesting opportunities across complex portfolios, considering wash sale rules and the interaction between different investment types. The rebalancing process has evolved to consider risk factors beyond simple asset class allocations, incorporating factors like interest rate sensitivity, inflation protection, and income generation potential.

Healthcare Cost Planning

Perhaps nowhere has AI made a more significant impact than in the complex realm of healthcare cost planning for retirement. Traditional retirement planning often treated healthcare costs as a simple inflation-adjusted estimate, but AI systems have introduced a level of sophistication that accounts for individual health factors, regional cost variations, and the complex interaction between different healthcare coverage options.

These systems analyze personal health data, family history, and lifestyle factors to create personalized healthcare cost projections. They can model different Medicare coverage scenarios, helping retirees optimize their coverage choices based on their specific health needs and financial situation. The integration of long-term care considerations has become more nuanced, with AI tools helping individuals decide not just whether to purchase long-term care insurance, but also when to buy it and what type of coverage best suits their circumstances.

Real-World Applications

Early Career Planning

The power of AI in retirement planning becomes evident even for those just beginning their careers. Young professionals often struggle to balance competing financial priorities—student loan repayment, housing costs, and retirement savings all vie for limited resources. AI systems help create clarity in this complexity by analyzing various scenarios and their long-term implications.

Consider the case of Maria Chen, a 26-year-old software engineer carrying $50,000 in student loan debt. Traditional advice might have simply encouraged her to start saving for retirement while paying down debt, but her AI planning tool provided much more nuanced guidance. The system analyzed her loan terms, career trajectory, and local cost of living to create a dynamic strategy that adjusted her retirement contributions based on her loan repayment progress. When she received performance bonuses, the AI recommended optimal splits between loan prepayment and retirement savings, considering factors like market conditions and tax implications.

Mid-Career Optimization

For established professionals in their 40s and 50s, AI retirement planning tools shine in their ability to optimize complex financial situations. These individuals often juggle multiple retirement accounts, investment properties, college savings for children, and peak earning years. The sophistication of AI analysis helps them make the most of these critical wealth-building years.

David Martinez, a 47-year-old physician, exemplifies how AI can transform mid-career retirement planning. His portfolio included a private practice 401(k), a hospital pension, multiple IRAs from previous employers, and a rental property. The AI system analyzed all these elements together, identifying opportunities for improved tax efficiency and suggesting account consolidation strategies. When his daughter began college applications, the system helped him balance education funding with retirement savings, creating a strategy that protected his retirement security while supporting his daughter's education.

Near-Retirement Planning

As retirement approaches, the complexity of financial decision-making often increases dramatically. AI systems have proven particularly valuable in this phase, helping soon-to-be retirees optimize crucial decisions that can impact their financial security for decades to come.

Take the example of Robert and Susan Baker, both 63 and planning to retire within two years. Their AI retirement platform analyzed dozens of Social Security claiming scenarios, considering their age difference, health status, and other income sources. The system identified a claiming strategy that would increase their lifetime benefits by over $100,000 compared to their original plan. Furthermore, it created a tax-efficient withdrawal strategy that would help them maintain their desired lifestyle while minimizing their tax burden throughout retirement.

The Future of AI in Retirement Planning

The evolution of AI in retirement planning continues at a rapid pace, with emerging technologies promising to make retirement planning even more personalized and effective. Virtual reality integration is on the horizon, allowing individuals to experience simulated versions of different retirement scenarios. This technology will enable people to make more informed decisions about retirement lifestyle choices by experiencing them virtually before making real-world commitments.

Genetic analysis is beginning to play a role in longevity predictions, with AI systems incorporating genetic markers and family health history to create more accurate lifespan projections. This information helps create more precise retirement planning strategies that better account for individual life expectancy and health-related costs.

The integration of real-time tax law analysis is becoming more sophisticated, with AI systems not just reacting to tax law changes but anticipating their likely impacts based on historical patterns and proposed legislation. This predictive capability helps retirees better position themselves for potential changes in the tax landscape.

Practical Implementation Guide

Successfully implementing AI retirement planning tools requires a thoughtful, systematic approach. The process begins with comprehensive data collection, but this goes far beyond simply gathering account statements. Modern AI systems can analyze spending patterns, health records, family history, and lifestyle preferences to create a complete financial picture.

The selection of appropriate AI tools requires careful consideration of several factors. Integration capabilities with existing financial accounts, security measures, and user interface design all play crucial roles in the tool's effectiveness. The best system for an individual depends on their specific needs, technical comfort level, and financial complexity.

Implementation should follow a structured approach, beginning with basic account connections and gradually expanding to more sophisticated features as users become comfortable with the system. Regular reviews and updates ensure the AI system maintains accurate information and continues to provide relevant recommendations as circumstances change.

Common Pitfalls to Avoid

While AI has transformed retirement planning, success requires avoiding several common pitfalls. Many users fall into the trap of over-reliance on automation without developing a basic understanding of retirement planning principles. This can lead to missed opportunities and potential mistakes when unusual circumstances arise that require human judgment.

Another common error is the insufficient input of personal information and preferences into AI systems. These tools can only provide accurate recommendations based on the quality of data they receive. Regular updates of personal information, financial circumstances, and retirement goals are crucial for maintaining the effectiveness of AI retirement planning tools.

Conclusion: Embracing AI for Retirement Success

The integration of AI into retirement planning represents a fundamental shift in how we prepare for our later years. These sophisticated tools have transformed retirement planning from a periodic review process into a dynamic, continuous optimization effort. However, success with AI retirement planning tools requires a balanced approach that combines technological capabilities with human wisdom and oversight.

The future of retirement planning lies in this thoughtful combination of AI capabilities with human insight. By embracing these tools while maintaining a clear understanding of our personal goals and values, we can create retirement strategies that are both sophisticated and personally meaningful. The key to success lies in using these tools consistently while maintaining the flexibility to adapt as circumstances change and new capabilities emerge.

As we look to the future, the role of AI in retirement planning will likely continue to expand and evolve. New technologies and capabilities will emerge, offering even more sophisticated ways to plan and prepare for retirement. However, the fundamental principle remains unchanged: AI tools are most effective when used as part of a thoughtful, comprehensive approach to retirement planning that considers both the numbers and the human elements of this crucial life transition.

Chapter 6:

Using AI for Debt Management

The Emotional and Financial Weight of Debt

While our previous chapter explored planning for retirement, many readers may find themselves facing a more immediate challenge: managing debt. If you're struggling with debt, know that you're not alone. Debt can feel overwhelming, affecting not just our financial health but our emotional well-being, relationships, and even physical health. The stress of debt can make it difficult to sleep, maintain relationships, or focus at work. It's crucial to understand that facing debt challenges doesn't reflect a personal failure—it's often the result of complex systemic factors, unexpected life events, or circumstances beyond our control.

Traditional approaches to debt management often added to this stress by requiring constant manual tracking, complex calculations, and difficult decisions about which debts to prioritize. Many people found themselves lying awake at night, trying to juggle payment dates, interest rates, and minimum payments while wondering if they were making the right choices. The emotional toll of these decisions can be exhausting, leading many to feel trapped in a cycle of debt that seems impossible to escape.

How AI Is Transforming the Debt Management Experience

A Compassionate Technological Partner

Modern AI debt management systems serve as more than just calculators—they act as patient, non-judgmental partners in your journey toward financial freedom. Unlike traditional financial advisors or debt counselors who might only be available during limited hours, AI systems provide 24/7 support and guidance.

They offer a safe space to explore your financial situation without fear of judgment or shame, helping you understand your options and develop a realistic path forward.

These systems understand that everyone's situation is unique. Whether you're dealing with student loans from pursuing higher education, medical debt from an unexpected illness, or credit card debt from a period of unemployment, AI tools can adapt their strategies to your specific circumstances and needs. They recognize that debt repayment isn't just about numbers—it's about creating a sustainable plan that works with your life.

Beyond Traditional Solutions

Consider Maria Gonzalez, a single mother working two jobs to support her family. Traditional debt advice suggested she should cut all discretionary spending— including the occasional movie night with her children— to maximize debt repayment. Her AI debt management system took a different approach, analyzing her spending patterns to find sustainable savings opportunities while preserving important family activities. The system identified utility optimization opportunities, discovered she was eligible for an income-based repayment program for her student loans, and helped her negotiate lower interest rates on her credit cards. These changes created breathing room in her budget without sacrificing her family's quality of life.

Understanding Modern AI Debt Management Features

Personalized Strategy Development

Today's AI debt management systems go far beyond simple payment calculations. They create comprehensive strategies that consider your entire financial picture, including:

Income Analysis: The system studies your income patterns, including regular paychecks, irregular earnings, and potential future changes. For gig workers or those with variable income, this might mean creating flexible payment plans that adjust automatically based on earnings.

Expense Evaluation: Rather than making blanket recommendations to cut spending, AI systems analyze your specific spending patterns to identify realistic opportunities for savings. They understand that some expenses, while technically discretionary, may be crucial for maintaining mental health and family relationships.

Life Event Integration: Modern AI systems can adjust your debt management strategy around major life events. Whether you're planning a wedding, expecting a child, or considering a career change, these systems help you balance debt repayment with other financial needs.

Stress-Reduction Through Automation

One of the most valuable aspects of AI debt management is its ability to reduce the mental load of debt management. These systems can:

Payment Automation: Schedule payments automatically while maintaining safe cushions in your accounts to prevent overdrafts.

Alert Systems: Provide early warnings about potential payment issues, giving you time to adjust rather than facing last-minute crises.

Progress Tracking: Offer encouraging updates about your debt repayment progress, helping maintain motivation during your financial journey.

Negotiation and Optimization

Modern AI systems can identify opportunities for improving your debt terms that you might not discover on your own. For example, when James Patterson's AI system analyzed his credit card debt, it identified that he qualified for a balance transfer offer that would provide 18 months at 0% interest. The system calculated the balance transfer fee and compared it to his potential interest savings, showing that this move would save him over $3,000 in interest charges.

Real-World Implementation: Starting Your Journey

Beginning with Compassion

The first step in implementing AI debt management is acknowledging your current situation with self-compassion. Many people delay seeking help because they feel shame about their debt. Remember that seeking help and using available tools shows wisdom and courage, not weakness.

When you first start using an AI debt management system, take time to:

Gather Your Information: Collect statements from all your debts, but don't feel overwhelmed if you can't find everything immediately. Many AI systems can help you identify debts through soft credit pulls that won't affect your credit score.

Share Your Story: Most AI systems now include features for explaining special circumstances or hardships. This information helps the system create more realistic and compassionate repayment strategies.

Set Realistic Expectations: Understand that debt repayment is a journey, not a sprint. Your AI system will help you create a sustainable, long-term strategy for financial freedom.

Creating Your Personal Strategy

Modern AI systems excel at creating flexible strategies that adapt to your life circumstances. They understand that rigid plans often fail and instead focus on creating resilient strategies that can weather life's uncertainties.

Take the case of David Chen, a teacher who started his debt repayment journey just before the COVID-19 pandemic hit. When schools closed and he faced unexpected technology expenses for remote teaching, his AI system quickly adapted his repayment strategy. It helped him identify emergency assistance programs, adjusted his payment schedules, and created a modified budget that accommodated his new circumstances while maintaining progress toward his financial goals.

Supporting Your Mental Health During Debt Repayment

The relationship between financial stress and mental health is profound and often overlooked in traditional debt management approaches. Research has consistently shown that individuals dealing with debt are three times more likely to experience anxiety and depression. Understanding this crucial connection, modern AI debt management systems have evolved to address not just the financial aspects of debt but also the psychological and emotional challenges that accompany it.

Integrated Wellness Approaches

Consider Sarah Mitchell's experience with anxiety-induced insomnia as she struggled with medical debt following an unexpected surgery. Traditional debt management tools focused solely on payment schedules and interest rates, leaving her to cope with the emotional burden alone. Her AI debt management system, however, noticed patterns in her late-night logins and irregular account checking that suggested high anxiety levels. The system began providing calming financial reassurance during these nighttime sessions, offering clear visualizations of her progress and gentle reminders of her successful payments to date.

Modern AI systems have developed sophisticated emotional intelligence capabilities that can recognize signs of financial distress through user interactions. When Thomas Rodriguez's system detected increasing frequency of budget checks and payment recalculations, it didn't just offer financial advice. Instead, it initiated a supportive dialogue about financial anxiety and provided resources for free financial counseling services in his area. This proactive approach helped Thomas address his concerns before they developed into more severe anxiety issues.

The celebration of progress has also evolved far beyond simple milestone notifications. These systems now create personalized "financial victory journals" that document not just numerical achievements but also the skills and resilience developed along the way. When Maria Gonzalez paid off her first credit card, her AI system created a detailed visualization of her journey, highlighting how she overcame specific challenges and developed new financial management skills. This documentation serves both as motivation and as a practical guide for tackling remaining debts.

Building Financial Resilience Through Emotional Intelligence

Modern AI systems understand that financial resilience is intrinsically linked to emotional resilience. They help users develop both through sophisticated behavioral psychology approaches integrated into their debt management strategies. For instance, when James

Patterson faced a setback after an unexpected car repair forced him to use his credit card, his AI system helped him understand that setbacks are a normal part of the debt repayment journey. Instead of just adjusting his payment schedule, the system helped him process the emotional impact of the setback and develop a stronger emergency fund strategy to prevent future stress.

These systems also recognize the importance of maintaining social connections during debt repayment. Many now include anonymous community features that allow users to share experiences and strategies while maintaining privacy. These communities are carefully moderated by AI to ensure they remain supportive and constructive, with the AI system actively identifying and promoting especially helpful success strategies and coping mechanisms shared by community members.

The Future of Compassionate AI Debt Management

As we look toward the future, the integration of artificial intelligence with debt management promises even more sophisticated and empathetic approaches to financial wellness. These developments aren't just about better algorithms or faster processing; they represent a fundamental shift in how we approach the human experience of dealing with debt.

Predictive Emotional Support Systems

Future AI systems will incorporate advanced emotional prediction models that can anticipate periods of financial stress before they become overwhelming. By analyzing patterns in spending, saving, and user interaction, these systems will provide preemptive emotional support and practical guidance. Imagine an

AI system that recognizes the approaching anniversary of a job loss that led to debt accumulation and proactively offers both emotional support and practical financial strategies for managing any associated anxiety.

The development of natural language processing capabilities will enable these systems to engage in more nuanced and emotionally intelligent conversations about financial challenges. Rather than simply providing data and recommendations, future AI systems will be able to engage in supportive dialogue that helps users process their emotions while working through financial decisions.

Enhanced Behavioral Understanding and Support

Future systems will develop increasingly sophisticated understanding of the behavioral patterns associated with financial stress and debt management. This might include analysis of voice patterns during voice-activated interactions, recognition of stress indicators in typing patterns, or even integration with wearable devices to monitor physical stress responses during financial planning sessions.

These insights will enable AI systems to create highly personalized intervention strategies. For example, if the system recognizes patterns indicating avoidance behavior around checking certain accounts, it might develop a graduated exposure approach, helping users face financial realities in manageable steps while providing emotional support and practical guidance throughout the process.

Holistic Family and Community Impact Analysis

The next generation of AI debt management systems will better understand and address the ripple effects of debt on families and communities. These systems will help users navigate the complex social dynamics of debt, from managing family financial discussions to understanding how debt repayment strategies might affect children's educational opportunities or family healthcare decisions.

Future AI systems will also be better equipped to understand and navigate cultural differences in attitudes toward debt and financial management. They will provide culturally sensitive guidance that respects different values and approaches to financial wellness while helping users work toward their debt repayment goals.

Integrated Life Planning
and Financial Wellness

Perhaps most significantly, future AI debt management systems will move beyond treating debt as an isolated problem to be solved. Instead, they will integrate debt management into a comprehensive life planning approach that considers career development, education opportunities, family planning, and long-term financial goals. These systems will help users understand how different life choices might impact their debt management journey and vice versa, enabling more informed and holistic decision-making.

By incorporating advanced scenario planning capabilities, these systems will help users visualize and understand the long-term implications of different debt management strategies in the context of their broader life goals. This might include modeling how different debt repayment approaches could affect retirement timing, housing opportunities, or children's education funding.

The future of AI debt management holds tremendous promise for creating more compassionate, effective, and personalized approaches to achieving financial freedom. As these technologies continue to evolve, they will provide increasingly sophisticated support for both the financial and emotional aspects of debt management, helping individuals not just eliminate debt but build lasting financial wellness and resilience.

Conclusion: Your Path to Financial Freedom

Remember that seeking help with debt management is a sign of strength, not weakness. Modern AI tools provide powerful allies in your journey toward financial freedom, offering sophisticated analysis and strategy development while maintaining sensitivity to the human aspects of debt management.

As you begin or continue your debt management journey, know that you're not alone. Millions of others have faced similar challenges and found their way to financial freedom. With the support of AI tools and a commitment to your financial well-being, you can create a path forward that works for your unique situation and leads to lasting financial health.

In our next chapter, we'll explore how AI can help you maintain and build upon your progress through personalized financial advice and planning strategies. The skills and habits you develop during debt management will serve as a foundation for building long-term financial success.

Chapter 7:

Personalized Financial Advice with AI

The Evolution of Financial Advice

As we've explored the transformative power of AI in retirement planning and debt management, we now turn to perhaps its most revolutionary application: personalized financial advice. The journey of financial guidance has evolved dramatically over the centuries, from the simple ledgers of medieval merchants to the complex algorithms of modern robo-advisors. Yet until recently, truly personalized financial advice remained a luxury available only to the wealthy, who could afford the services of experienced financial advisors charging thousands of dollars annually.

Traditional financial advice often resembled a one-size-fits-all garment that never quite fit anyone perfectly. Financial advisors, constrained by time and human cognitive limitations, typically sorted clients into broad categories based on age, income, and basic risk tolerance. While this approach provided general guidance, it failed to account for the intricate tapestry of individual circumstances, goals, and values that make each person's financial journey unique.

The AI Revolution in Personal Finance

Beyond Traditional Boundaries

Modern AI-powered financial advisory systems represent a fundamental shift in how we approach personal finance. These sophisticated platforms analyze hundreds of variables simultaneously, creating financial strategies as unique as fingerprints. Consider the experience of Maria Chen, a 34-year-old digital nomad whose irregular income from multiple international sources had left traditional financial advisors puzzled. Her AI financial advisor analyzed her complex income patterns, cross-border tax implications, and location-dependent expenses to create a flexible financial strategy that adapted as she moved between countries.

The system didn't just account for the obvious variables like income and expenses—it considered factors such as local cost-of-living adjustments, currency exchange rate trends, and even the seasonal nature of her freelance work. When Maria decided to spend three months in Bali, her AI advisor automatically adjusted her budget to account for lower living costs while increasing her retirement contributions to take advantage of the reduced expenses.

The Power of Continuous Adaptation

Unlike traditional financial advice that might be reviewed annually or quarterly, AI systems provide continuous, real-time adjustments to your financial strategy. Take the case of James and Sarah Peterson, who received life-changing news one Tuesday morning—they were expecting twins. Within minutes of entering this information into their AI financial planning system, it began recalibrating their entire financial strategy. The system analyzed:

The impact on their housing needs and potential relocation costs:

- Adjustments to their insurance coverage and healthcare planning
- Modified retirement contribution strategies to balance long-term savings with new short-term needs
- Updated tax planning to maximize new deductions and credits
- Revised emergency fund requirements for a larger family

The system didn't just crunch numbers—it provided context and explanations for each recommendation, helping James and Sarah understand the reasoning behind the suggested changes. This transparency helped them make informed decisions about their financial future while feeling confident in their choices.

The Architecture of Personalized AI Financial Planning

Dynamic Goal Integration

Modern AI financial planning systems have transformed how we approach goal setting and achievement. Rather than treating financial goals as fixed targets, these systems understand that goals exist within a complex web of interdependencies and life circumstances.

Consider the experience of David Martinez, a 45-year-old teacher who dreamed of opening a small bookstore in retirement. Traditional financial planning might have simply calculated the capital needed and created a savings target. His AI financial advisor, however, took a more nuanced approach:

It analyzed local real estate trends in areas suitable for bookstores:

- Evaluated the impact of various funding options, from loans to retirement account withdrawals
- Considered how different timeline scenarios would affect his pension benefits

- Suggested relevant skills development opportunities that could help reduce future operating costs
- Created flexible savings strategies that adapted to his changing circumstances

When David's daughter decided to attend graduate school, the system didn't simply push back his bookstore timeline. Instead, it analyzed multiple scenarios for supporting his daughter's education while maintaining progress toward his business goal, ultimately suggesting a hybrid approach that kept both dreams alive.

Life Event Prediction and Adaptation

One of the most sophisticated aspects of modern AI financial planning is its ability to anticipate and prepare for life events before they occur. These systems analyze patterns in your financial behavior, life circumstances, and broader demographic trends to predict potential future events and their financial implications.

Lisa Chang's experience illustrates this capability perfectly. Her AI financial advisor noticed subtle changes in her spending patterns—increased browsing of real estate websites, higher savings rates, and research into school districts. The system recognized these as potential indicators of an upcoming home purchase decision and proactively began:

- Analyzing her credit profile and suggesting improvements to secure better mortgage rates
- Evaluating different neighborhoods based on her browsing history and financial capabilities
- Calculating optimal down payment scenarios based on her savings rate and investment returns
- Suggesting modifications to her investment portfolio to ensure appropriate liquidity
- Creating contingency plans for various housing market scenarios

When Lisa did decide to start house hunting six months later, she was already optimally positioned for the purchase, thanks to her AI advisor's predictive capabilities.

Advanced Financial Optimization

The Integration of Multiple Financial Dimensions

Modern AI financial advisors have revolutionized how we approach financial optimization by recognizing the intricate web of relationships between various aspects of our financial lives. Think of your financial life as a complex ecosystem where every decision creates ripples that affect multiple areas simultaneously. Traditional financial advisors, limited by human cognitive capabilities, often had to break down this ecosystem into manageable chunks, potentially missing important interactions between different financial domains.

Consider how a seemingly simple decision about increasing your 401(k) contribution might affect your ability to save for a home down payment, impact your tax situation, influence your debt repayment strategy, and even affect your insurance needs. AI systems excel at modeling these complex interdependencies in real-time, creating truly optimized strategies that account for all these moving parts.

Take the case of Michael Wong, a 38-year-old software engineer who received a significant promotion. Traditional advice might have simply suggested increasing his retirement contributions. His AI financial advisor, however, conducted a comprehensive analysis that revealed surprising insights about the interconnected nature of his financial life. The system identified that by coordinating multiple financial moves in a specific sequence, Michael could achieve significantly better outcomes:

First, it analyzed the optimal timing for exercising his stock options, considering not just the current stock price but also his projected income levels, tax brackets, and alternative minimum tax (AMT) exposure over the next several years. The system then connected this analysis to his charitable giving goals, recognizing an opportunity to donate appreciated shares to a donor-advised fund. This strategy would not only provide immediate tax benefits but also create a sustainable long-term philanthropic strategy.

The AI didn't stop there. It recognized that the tax savings from this strategy could be strategically reinvested, creating a positive feedback loop in Michael's financial ecosystem. By modeling thousands of possible scenarios, the system identified that using the tax savings to fund a health savings account (HSA) would provide the best combination of tax advantages, healthcare cost coverage, and long-term investment potential.

Advanced Tax Strategy Integration

The optimization of tax outcomes has evolved far beyond simple deduction identification. Modern AI systems approach tax strategy as a dynamic, multi-year optimization problem that connects to every aspect of your financial life. These systems constantly monitor changing tax laws, court decisions, and IRS guidance to identify opportunities and risks in real-time.

Consider Rachel Stevens, a freelance graphic designer who also earned income from a small Etsy shop. Her AI advisor didn't just notice that her Etsy income was approaching a crucial tax threshold – it created a sophisticated multi-year strategy to optimize her entire tax situation. The system analyzed:

Tax Bracket Management: It identified opportunities to shift income between tax years to maintain optimal tax brackets, considering both federal and state tax implications.

Business Structure Optimization: Rather than simply suggesting an LLC or S-corporation, the system modeled multiple business structure scenarios across a ten-year period. It considered factors such as:
-   The projected growth rate of her business
-   Potential future expansion into new product lines
-   Healthcare coverage options under different business structures
-   Retirement plan options and their tax implications
-   State-specific tax treatment of different entity types
-   Potential future exit strategies

Retirement Account Optimization: The system created a dynamic retirement account strategy that adjusted based on her income fluctuations. During high-income months, it recommended higher contributions to tax-advantaged accounts, while maintaining flexibility for leaner periods.

Healthcare Tax Integration: The AI recognized that Rachel's variable income made her eligible for premium tax credits on her health insurance in certain months. It created a sophisticated strategy to manage her income timing to optimize these credits while maintaining business growth.

When mid-year tax law changes occurred, the system didn't simply recalculate existing strategies – it performed a complete reanalysis of all possible scenarios under the new rules.
This included:

- Modelling the impact of new tax provisions on different business structures
- Identifying new planning opportunities created by the changes
- Adjusting timing strategies for income and expenses
- Recalibrating retirement contribution recommendations

- Updating healthcare coverage optimization strategies

Dynamic Asset Location and Investment Tax Efficiency

Modern AI systems have transformed the concept of asset location – the practice of placing investments in accounts with the most advantageous tax treatment. These systems continuously monitor and adjust investment placements across accounts, considering factors such as:

Tax Bracket Arbitrage: The system analyzes current and future expected tax brackets to optimize the timing of taxable events.

Wash Sale Management: AI advisors can coordinate trading across all accounts, including IRAs and spousal accounts, to harvest tax losses while maintaining desired investment exposure and avoiding wash sale rules.

Dividend Tax Optimization: The system places investments with different dividend characteristics (qualified vs. non-qualified) in the most tax-advantaged locations while maintaining overall portfolio balance.

The Future of Personalized Financial Advice

Integration of Environmental and Social Factors

The next generation of AI financial advisors will incorporate an even broader range of factors into their analysis. These systems are beginning to consider:

Environmental Impact: Analyzing the carbon footprint of investment choices and suggesting sustainable alternatives that align with both financial goals and environmental values.

Social Responsibility: Evaluating companies' labor practices, community impact, and ethical standards as part of investment recommendations.

Personal Values Alignment: Creating financial strategies that balance monetary returns with individual values and social impact goals.

Enhanced Predictive Capabilities

Future AI systems will leverage advanced predictive models to anticipate and prepare for an even wider range of life events and financial scenarios. These might include:

Career Path Optimization: Analyzing labor market trends and personal skills to suggest career moves that maximize long-term financial outcomes.

Health-Finance Integration: Incorporating genetic and lifestyle factors to better predict and plan for future healthcare needs and costs.

Family Planning Support: Providing sophisticated modeling of different family planning scenarios and their financial implications.

Implementation Strategies for Success

Getting Started with AI Financial Advice

The journey to successful AI-powered financial planning begins with thoughtful preparation and implementation. Here's how to approach it:

First, gather comprehensive financial information, including:

- All income sources and their patterns
- Complete debt and asset pictures
- Insurance coverage details
- Family financial obligations
- Long-term goals and aspirations

Next, select an AI advisory platform that aligns with your specific needs. Consider factors such as:

- The complexity of your financial situation
- Your comfort with technology
- The level of human support available if needed

- The platform's track record and security
measures

Maintaining Success Over Time

Long-term success with AI financial planning requires
ongoing engagement and periodic review. Regular
check-ins help ensure your financial strategy remains
aligned with your evolving goals and circumstances.
Set aside time each month to:

Review the AI's recommendations and understand their
rationale
Update the system with any significant life changes
Evaluate progress toward your financial goals
Learn from the educational content provided

Conclusion: The Future of Financial Planning

As we look to the future, the role of AI in personal
financial planning will continue to expand and evolve.
These systems will become even more sophisticated in
their ability to understand and adapt to individual

circumstances, while maintaining the crucial balance between automation and personal touch.

The true power of AI financial planning lies not just in its ability to crunch numbers and optimize strategies, but in its capacity to democratize sophisticated financial advice. What was once available only to the wealthy is now accessible to anyone with a smartphone, marking a fundamental shift in how we approach personal finance.

As we move forward, the key to success will be learning to work effectively with these AI systems—understanding their capabilities and limitations, providing them with accurate information, and using their insights to make better financial decisions. The future of financial planning is not about replacing human judgment with artificial intelligence, but about creating a powerful partnership that enhances our ability to achieve our financial goals.

In our next chapter, we'll explore how AI can help you navigate the complexities of market analysis and

investment timing, building on the personalized
foundation we've established here.

Chapter 8:

Predicting Market Trends with AI

The Evolution of Market Prediction

Throughout history, investors have sought to unlock the secrets of market movements, searching for patterns in everything from weather reports to sunspot activity. In the bustling trading floors of the early 20th century, success often depended on access to information—who could get tomorrow's news today. As we moved into the digital age, algorithmic trading introduced new levels of sophistication, but even these systems were limited by their rigid, rule-based nature. The emergence of artificial intelligence has ushered in a new era of market analysis, one where machines can process and learn from vast amounts of data in ways that transform our understanding of market dynamics.

Understanding Market Complexity

To appreciate the revolutionary nature of AI in market prediction, we must first understand the extraordinary complexity of financial markets. Every second, countless variables influence market movements: corporate earnings reports, geopolitical events, natural disasters, social media trends, and even human emotions all play their part. Traditional analysis methods struggled to process this complexity, often focusing on a limited set of variables while missing crucial interconnections.

Consider the challenge faced by Sarah Chen, a retail investor trying to evaluate a potential investment in an electric vehicle company. Traditional analysis might have focused primarily on the company's financial statements and industry reports. However, the true picture of the company's prospects involved a far more complex web of factors: global supply chain dynamics, technological advances in battery technology, changing consumer preferences, environmental regulations across different countries, and the competitive landscape of both traditional automakers and new entrants.

Modern AI Market Analysis

The Power of Multi-Dimensional Analysis

Today's AI systems approach market analysis with unprecedented sophistication, simultaneously evaluating multiple dimensions of market influence. Let's explore how these systems work through the experience of Marcus Thompson, a mid-career professional managing his retirement portfolio.

Marcus was considering increasing his investment in renewable energy stocks. His AI analysis platform didn't simply examine historical price trends and financial statements. Instead, it conducted a comprehensive analysis that included:

Global Policy Analysis: The system monitored and interpreted environmental legislation and energy policies across major economies, understanding how regulatory changes might impact different segments of the renewable energy sector.

Technology Assessment: By analyzing patent filings, research papers, and technical documentation, the AI evaluated the technological readiness of different renewable energy solutions and their potential market impact.

Supply Chain Intelligence: The system mapped complex global supply networks, identifying potential bottlenecks and opportunities in the renewable energy supply chain.

Social Sentiment Analysis: Advanced natural language processing monitored social media, news articles, and industry forums to gauge changing public attitudes toward different renewable energy technologies.

The AI system synthesized these diverse inputs into actionable insights, helping Marcus understand not just whether to invest, but also which segments of the renewable energy sector showed the most promise and what risks to monitor.

Real-Time Adaptation and Learning

Modern AI market prediction systems don't just analyze static data—they learn and adapt in real-time. When a major solar panel manufacturer announced a technological breakthrough, Marcus's AI system didn't simply note the news. It:

Analyzed the technical details of the breakthrough against its database of existing technologies
Evaluated the potential impact on competing technologies and companies
Assessed the credibility of the claims based on the company's previous announcements
Monitored initial market reactions and technical expert responses
Adjusted its sector outlook based on this new information

This dynamic learning capability represents a fundamental shift from traditional market analysis tools. Rather than relying on fixed rules or historical patterns, AI systems continuously refine their understanding of market dynamics.

The Science Behind
AI Market Prediction

Natural Language Processing
and Sentiment Analysis

One of the most powerful capabilities of modern AI
market prediction systems is their ability to understand
and analyze human language. These systems process
millions of news articles, social media posts, earnings
call transcripts, and regulatory filings each day,
extracting nuanced insights about market sentiment
and trends.

Consider how this worked during a recent earnings
season. Traditional analysis might focus on headline
numbers like revenue and earnings per share. The AI
system that Thomas Rodriguez used, however, went
much deeper:

Earnings Call Analysis: The system analyzed not just
what was said during earnings calls, but how it was

said, detecting subtle changes in executive language patterns that might indicate confidence or concern.

Supply Chain Insights: By processing thousands of local news reports and social media posts, the system identified potential supply chain disruptions before they were widely reported.

Competitive Intelligence: The AI monitored job postings, patent applications, and technical documentation to understand how companies were positioning themselves for future growth.

Pattern Recognition and Anomaly Detection

Modern AI systems excel at identifying subtle patterns and anomalies that human analysts might miss. These systems can:

Detect Statistical Anomalies: By analyzing millions of data points, AI can identify when market behavior deviates from historical norms in statistically significant ways.

Recognize Complex Patterns: The systems can identify intricate relationships between seemingly unrelated market events and conditions.

Predict Potential Disruptions: By synthesizing multiple data sources, AI can often detect early warning signs of market shifts.

Let's see how this worked in practice through the experience of Jennifer Chang, a small business owner investing for her company's future. Her AI system identified an unusual pattern in semiconductor industry suppliers—subtle changes in order patterns and inventory levels that suggested a potential supply shortage. This insight allowed Jennifer to adjust her technology sector investments months before the shortage became widely known.

Implementation Strategies for AI Market Analysis

Building a Robust Analysis Framework

Successfully implementing AI market prediction tools requires a thoughtful, systematic approach that goes beyond simply following buy and sell signals. The key is to create a framework that integrates AI insights with your overall investment strategy while maintaining a clear understanding of the technology's capabilities and limitations.

Consider the experience of Robert Martinez, a retired engineer who initially struggled to effectively use AI market prediction tools. Like many investors, he initially viewed AI as a crystal ball that would tell him exactly when to buy and sell. After several disappointing trades, he worked with his AI platform to develop a more sophisticated approach:

Foundation Building: Rather than jumping straight into trading, Robert spent time understanding how his AI system analyzed different types of market data. He learned to:

- Interpret confidence levels in AI predictions

- Understand the types of data feeding into different analyses
- Recognize when market conditions might be outside the AI's training parameters
- Differentiate between short-term trading signals and long-term trend analysis

Integration Strategy: Robert developed a systematic approach to incorporating AI insights into his investment decisions:
- Created a checklist for validating AI recommendations against his investment goals
- Established clear criteria for when to act on AI signals and when to seek additional validation
- Developed a journaling system to track the effectiveness of different types of AI predictions

Risk Management in AI-Driven Trading

The implementation of AI market prediction tools must include robust risk management protocols. Modern AI systems approach risk management through multiple layers:

Position Sizing in Modern AI Systems

The approach to position sizing in modern AI trading systems represents a significant advancement over traditional methods. Rather than relying on simple percentage-based allocations, these systems employ sophisticated multi-factor analysis to determine optimal position sizes. They begin by examining historical volatility patterns, not just of individual securities but of entire market sectors and their interrelationships. This analysis extends beyond simple standard deviation calculations to include jump risk, tail risk, and regime-dependent volatility patterns.

The systems then evaluate how potential positions correlate with existing portfolio holdings, using advanced statistical techniques to identify hidden correlations that might only emerge during market stress. This correlation analysis goes deeper than traditional metrics, examining how relationships between assets evolve under different market conditions and economic scenarios.

Current market conditions play a crucial role in position sizing decisions. The AI systems continuously monitor market sentiment, liquidity conditions, and trading volumes to adjust position sizes dynamically. During periods of market stress, when liquidity might become constrained, the systems automatically adjust position sizes to maintain manageable risk levels.

Perhaps most importantly, these systems consider individual risk tolerance and financial circumstances in a highly nuanced way. Rather than using simple risk tolerance questionnaires, they analyze actual trading behavior, portfolio decisions, and responses to market movements to build a dynamic risk profile that evolves with the investor's experience and changing financial situation.

Scenario Analysis in AI Trading

Modern AI trading systems have transformed scenario analysis from a periodic exercise into a continuous, dynamic process. These systems run thousands of scenario simulations in real-time, constantly updating their analysis as market conditions change. The stress testing process examines not just historical market crashes but also synthesizes potential future scenarios based on current market conditions and emerging risks.

The systems create sophisticated models that analyze how portfolios might perform under various economic scenarios. These scenarios go beyond simple market up/down simulations to include complex combinations of factors such as inflation regimes, interest rate environments, geopolitical events, and technological disruptions. The AI considers how these factors might interact and compound each other, creating more realistic stress tests than traditional methods.

A particularly valuable aspect of modern AI scenario analysis is its ability to examine correlation breakdown during market stress. The systems understand that historical correlations often fail during crisis periods and model how these breakdowns might affect portfolio performance. This analysis helps investors prepare for scenarios where traditional diversification strategies might prove less effective than expected.

Risk Monitoring Evolution

The evolution of risk monitoring in AI systems represents a quantum leap forward in portfolio management. These systems perform continuous, real-time assessment of portfolio risks, analyzing everything from market risk to liquidity risk to counterparty risk. The monitoring process adapts to changing market conditions, automatically adjusting risk parameters based on market volatility, trading volumes, and other relevant factors.

Position sizes receive constant evaluation and adjustment based on evolving market conditions. The AI systems track not just absolute position sizes but also their relative importance in the portfolio context. They consider factors such as sector concentration, factor exposures, and potential liquidation impact when determining whether positions need adjustment.

The early warning systems developed by modern AI platforms go far beyond simple price alerts. They monitor a complex web of market indicators, news flows, and trading patterns to identify potential risks before they fully materialize. These systems can detect subtle changes in market behavior that might signal developing problems, allowing investors to take preventive action rather than reacting to already-manifested risks.

Clinical Trial Analysis in Modern AI Systems

The analysis of clinical trials has become one of the most sophisticated applications of AI in market prediction. Modern systems employ advanced natural language processing and machine learning techniques to monitor and analyze the complex landscape of medical research. These systems track not just the basic progress of clinical trials but conduct deep analysis of trial designs, patient populations, and statistical methodologies to assess the likelihood of success.

Patient recruitment rates receive particular attention in these analyses, as they often provide early indicators of trial success or potential problems. The AI systems analyze historical recruitment patterns in similar trials, considering factors such as disease type, trial complexity, and geographic location to identify potential delays or acceleration in trial progress. This analysis extends to examining the relationships between recruitment rates and ultimate trial outcomes, helping investors better understand the significance of recruitment developments.

The historical success patterns in similar trials provide crucial context for current trial analysis. AI systems maintain extensive databases of historical trial results, categorizing them by therapeutic area, trial design, patient population, and numerous other factors. This historical analysis helps identify which characteristics are most predictive of trial success, allowing for more accurate assessment of current trials.

Patent Landscape Analysis

The examination of patent landscapes by AI systems represents a fundamental shift in how we understand technological development in various industries. These systems go far beyond simple patent counting to create sophisticated maps of technological evolution and competitive positioning. They analyze not just patent applications and approvals but the complex web of citations that connect different technologies and innovations.

Citation network analysis has become particularly powerful in understanding technological relationships and potential market impacts. AI systems trace how innovations build upon each other, identifying which patents serve as fundamental building blocks for subsequent developments. This analysis helps investors understand which companies hold truly foundational intellectual property and which might be more vulnerable to technological obsolescence.

The competitive positioning analysis derived from patent data provides crucial insights into market opportunities and risks. AI systems examine how different companies' patent portfolios overlap and interact, identifying potential areas of future competition or collaboration. They also analyze the quality and breadth of patent protection, helping investors understand which companies have built the strongest defensive positions around their intellectual property.

Global Market Integration Analysis

The analysis of global market integration has reached new levels of sophistication with modern AI systems. Currency dynamics receive particularly detailed attention, with systems monitoring not just exchange rate movements but the complex interplay of factors that influence currency values. These analyses incorporate central bank policies, economic indicators, and capital flows to create comprehensive models of currency behavior and its market impact.

Political risk assessment has evolved far beyond simple stability metrics. AI systems now analyze vast amounts of news, social media, and government communications to create nuanced understanding of political developments and their market implications. They track policy changes and their implementation, understanding how different political scenarios might affect market outcomes.

The analysis of economic integration has become increasingly sophisticated, with AI systems mapping complex networks of trade relationships and supply chain dependencies. These systems understand how disruptions in one market might cascade through the global economic system, helping investors anticipate and prepare for potential market impacts. They analyze cross-border capital flows not just in terms of volume but also in terms of their stability and potential for sudden shifts.

Future Technology Integration

The future of AI market prediction promises even more sophisticated capabilities as new technologies emerge and mature. The integration of quantum computing represents a particularly exciting frontier. As quantum systems become more accessible, they will enable AI systems to process and analyze data at unprecedented scales. This quantum advantage will allow for the modeling of vastly more complex market scenarios and the identification of subtle patterns that remain invisible to current systems.

The enhancement of natural language understanding capabilities will transform how AI systems interpret market-relevant information. Future systems will better grasp cultural nuances in different markets, understanding how local customs and communication styles might affect market behavior. They will develop deeper appreciation for implicit meaning in corporate communications, reading between the lines of official statements to better understand company prospects and market dynamics.

The development of long-term narrative understanding will allow AI systems to track how market stories evolve over time, recognizing how changing narratives might signal shifts in market sentiment and direction. This capability will help investors better understand the psychological factors that often drive market movements.

The evolution of visualization and interaction capabilities will transform how investors engage with market data and AI insights. Virtual reality market visualization will allow investors to literally walk through market data, examining relationships and patterns in intuitive, three-dimensional spaces. Interactive scenario testing will enable investors to explore different market possibilities in real-time, adjusting strategies based on immediate feedback from AI systems.

Ethical Considerations in Market Efficiency

The increasing power of AI market prediction tools raises important questions about market efficiency and fairness. The challenge of monitoring for potential market manipulation has become more complex as AI systems become more sophisticated. Modern systems must constantly evaluate whether their predictions and trading recommendations might inadvertently contribute to market distortions.

The issue of fair access to AI capabilities has emerged as a crucial consideration in market democracy. As these tools become more powerful, ensuring that they remain accessible to retail investors becomes increasingly important for maintaining market fairness. This challenge extends beyond simple access to include the need for appropriate education and training to help investors effectively use these sophisticated tools.

The transparency of AI decision-making processes represents another crucial ethical consideration. As these systems become more complex, maintaining clear understanding of how they reach their conclusions becomes both more important and more challenging. The industry must balance the need for sophisticated analysis with the requirement for explainable, understandable decision-making processes that investors can trust and verify.

Educational Integration or Market Understanding

The development of educational capabilities in AI market prediction systems represents a crucial evolution in their functionality. These systems must not only provide sophisticated analysis but also help investors understand the reasoning behind their predictions and recommendations. This educational component includes detailed explanations of analytical methods, clear presentation of supporting evidence, and guidance on how to effectively incorporate AI insights into investment decisions.

The future of market analysis lies in this thoughtful integration of advanced AI capabilities with human understanding and judgment. Success will depend not just on the power of AI algorithms but on our ability to use these tools wisely and ethically, maintaining market integrity while advancing our ability to understand and navigate complex financial markets.

Advanced Applications of AI in Market Analysis

Sector-Specific Intelligence in Healthcare Markets

The application of AI analysis to specific market sectors has reached unprecedented levels of sophistication, particularly in complex industries like healthcare. Maria Chen's experience investing in biotechnology companies illustrates how modern AI systems approach sector-specific analysis. When Maria began exploring biotech investments, her AI system developed a comprehensive analytical framework that considered multiple layers of industry-specific factors.

In the realm of clinical trials, the system conducted continuous, deep analysis of ongoing research across the industry. This analysis went far beyond simple tracking of trial progress. The system examined the intricate details of patient recruitment patterns, understanding how variations in recruitment rates might signal potential issues or opportunities. By analyzing historical data from thousands of previous trials, the system identified subtle patterns that often preceded successful trial outcomes. These patterns considered factors such as the complexity of the trial protocol, the specific disease being studied, and the demographic characteristics of the patient population.

The examination of patent landscapes revealed complex networks of innovation and competition within the biotechnology sector. The system tracked not just patent applications and approvals but analyzed the relationships between different technologies through citation networks. This analysis helped identify which companies held foundational patents that might prove crucial for future developments. The system could determine when new patent applications might represent significant technological breakthroughs versus incremental improvements, providing crucial insights for investment decisions.

Regulatory intelligence in healthcare markets requires particularly sophisticated analysis. The AI system maintained comprehensive databases of FDA communications, policy developments, and historical approval patterns. It could identify subtle shifts in regulatory language that might signal changing attitudes toward certain types of treatments or technologies. The analysis of historical approval patterns proved especially valuable, as it helped predict how regulators might approach novel treatments based on their handling of similar innovations in the past.

Global Market Integration Dynamics

The complexity of global markets demands equally sophisticated analysis tools. James Wilson's experience investing in emerging markets demonstrates how modern AI systems approach global market analysis. Rather than treating markets as isolated entities, these systems understand the intricate web of relationships that connect different economies and financial markets.

Currency analysis in the modern era extends far beyond simple exchange rate tracking. AI systems examine the complex interplay between monetary policy, economic indicators, and market sentiment that drives currency movements. They analyze central bank communications not just for explicit policy statements but for subtle shifts in tone that might signal future policy changes. The systems track currency flow patterns across different market segments, identifying when unusual movements might signal emerging trends or potential market stress.

Political risk assessment has evolved into a nuanced analysis of multiple factors that might affect market stability. Modern AI systems analyze everything from social media sentiment to economic policy proposals to understand how political developments might impact markets. They track not just official policy announcements but also the public response to these policies, understanding how social sentiment might influence their implementation and effectiveness.

The Quantum Future of Market Analysis

The integration of quantum computing represents perhaps the most exciting frontier in AI market prediction. As quantum systems become more accessible, they will fundamentally transform our ability to analyze and understand markets. These systems will process vastly larger datasets in real-time, enabling analysis of market relationships that remain invisible to current technologies. The ability to model more complex market scenarios will allow investors to better understand potential outcomes and risks.

The enhanced pattern recognition capabilities of quantum-powered AI will reveal subtle market relationships that current systems cannot detect. These might include complex correlations between seemingly unrelated market factors or early warning signs of major market shifts. The integration of quantum computing will also enable more sophisticated risk analysis, helping investors better understand and manage potential market risks.

The Evolution of Market Understanding

The future of market analysis through AI will feature dramatically enhanced natural language understanding capabilities. These systems will grasp not just the literal meaning of market communications but the subtle cultural nuances that often influence market behavior in different regions. They will better understand how corporate communications might signal future developments, reading between the lines of official statements to identify potential opportunities or risks.

This enhanced understanding will extend to long-term narrative analysis, tracking how market stories develop and evolve over time. The systems will recognize how changing narratives might signal shifts in market sentiment or direction, helping investors anticipate and prepare for market changes.

The Ethical Dimension of AI Market Analysis

The increasing sophistication of AI market prediction tools raises important ethical considerations about market efficiency and fairness. The challenge of maintaining market integrity grows more complex as these tools become more powerful. Modern systems must carefully monitor for potential market manipulation, ensuring that their predictions and trading recommendations don't inadvertently create or amplify market distortions.

The democratization of access to sophisticated market analysis tools represents another crucial ethical consideration. As these systems become more powerful, ensuring they remain accessible to retail investors becomes increasingly important for maintaining market fairness. This accessibility must include not just the tools themselves but also comprehensive education about their capabilities and limitations.

The transparency of AI decision-making processes in market analysis represents a crucial challenge. As these systems become more complex, maintaining clear understanding of how they reach their conclusions becomes both more important and more difficult. The industry must balance the power of sophisticated analysis with the need for explainable, verifiable decision-making processes that investors can trust and understand.

Conclusion: The Human-AI Partnership in Market Analysis

As we look toward the future of market analysis, the key to success lies in effectively combining the power of AI analysis with human judgment and experience. While AI systems can process vast amounts of data and identify subtle patterns, human investors bring crucial context and wisdom to the investment process. The most successful investors will be those who learn to leverage AI capabilities while maintaining a strong foundation in fundamental investment principles.

This partnership between human insight and AI capabilities represents the future of market analysis. As we move forward, the challenge will be to harness the growing power of AI tools while maintaining the human judgment and wisdom necessary for successful investing. The next chapter will explore how these same principles apply to real estate investing, where AI analysis meets the unique challenges of property markets.

Chapter 9:

AI in Real Estate Investing

The Evolution of Real Estate Analysis

Real estate investment has traditionally relied heavily on human intuition and local market knowledge. Successful investors often spent years developing an almost sixth sense about which neighborhoods would appreciate and which properties held hidden value. While this expertise remains valuable, the emergence of artificial intelligence has transformed how we evaluate and select real estate investments. This revolution in property analysis represents perhaps the most significant change in real estate investing since the introduction of mortgage-backed securities.

Consider how real estate decisions were made just a decade ago. Investors would drive through neighborhoods, talk to local agents, and pore over basic demographic data and recent sales figures. While these methods could prove effective, they were limited by human cognitive capacity and often influenced by personal biases. Today's AI-powered analysis systems bring unprecedented precision and objectivity to these evaluations, processing vast amounts of data to identify opportunities that human analysis might miss.

The Multi-Dimensional Nature of Modern Property Analysis

Property Valuation in the AI Era

Traditional property valuation relied heavily on comparable sales, often called "comps," with adjustments made for obvious differences in property features. Modern AI valuation systems have transformed this process into a sophisticated multi-factor analysis that considers hundreds of variables simultaneously. These systems examine not just obvious factors like square footage and number of bedrooms, but also subtle influences on property value that traditional analysis might overlook.

Consider the experience of Sarah Chen, a first-time investor who recently used an AI system to evaluate properties in Seattle's rapidly changing market. The system identified a property that traditional analysis had overlooked because its comparable sales appeared unfavorable. However, the AI recognized several subtle factors that suggested significant appreciation potential:

The system analyzed thousands of geotagged social media posts to identify emerging neighborhood trends, noting increasing mentions of new restaurants and cultural venues in the area. It examined satellite imagery over time to track physical improvements in the neighborhood, from new construction to street repairs and landscaping projects. The AI even analyzed sound level data from city sensors to identify areas where traffic noise was decreasing due to recent infrastructure improvements.

Dynamic Rental Market Analysis

The analysis of rental markets has evolved far beyond simple supply and demand metrics. Modern AI systems create sophisticated models of rental market dynamics that consider multiple timeframes and market segments simultaneously. These systems can predict not just current market rates but future rental demand patterns based on an extraordinary range of factors.

James Rodriguez's experience with a rental property investment in Austin illustrates this sophistication. When evaluating potential rental properties, his AI system conducted a comprehensive analysis that included:

The system began by examining traditional factors like local employment trends and population growth. However, it went much deeper, analyzing company registration data to identify emerging startup clusters that might drive future rental demand. It examined building permit applications to forecast future housing supply, and analyzed rideshare data to understand changing transportation patterns that might affect property desirability.

The AI also identified subtle seasonal patterns in rental demand specific to different Austin neighborhoods. It discovered that properties near certain tech corridors commanded premium rents during summer months when internship programs peaked, while other areas showed stronger winter rental markets due to university schedules.

Neighborhood Evolution Prediction

Perhaps the most impressive capability of modern AI real estate systems is their ability to predict neighborhood development patterns. These systems have transformed the identification of up-and-coming areas from an art into a data-driven science, though one that still benefits from human insight and local knowledge.

Consider how these systems analyzed the transformation of a former industrial district in Portland. The AI examined dozens of potential indicators of neighborhood change:

The system tracked business license applications to identify emerging commercial clusters. It analyzed renovation permit applications to spot early signs of property improvement trends. Social media sentiment analysis revealed changing perceptions of the neighborhood among different demographic groups. The AI even examined food delivery app data to identify areas seeing increases in restaurant variety and quality.

This multi-dimensional analysis helped investors identify opportunities months or even years before traditional market indicators would have revealed them. However, the system didn't just identify broad trends – it provided nuanced analysis of how different properties might benefit from these changes based on their specific characteristics and locations.

Advanced Property Analysis Techniques

The evolution of AI in real estate has introduced sophisticated analytical capabilities that transform how we evaluate individual properties. These systems go far beyond traditional metrics like square footage and number of bedrooms, examining properties through multiple analytical lenses simultaneously.

Michael Chang's recent experience searching for a multi-family investment property in Chicago illustrates these advanced capabilities. The AI system he used conducted a comprehensive property analysis that considered both physical characteristics and market positioning. It began by analyzing the building's structural elements using AI interpretation of city inspection records, permit histories, and even satellite imagery to assess roof condition and drainage patterns.

The system then examined the property's energy efficiency potential, using weather data and architectural analysis to model potential improvements. It identified specific upgrades that would offer the best return on investment, considering factors like local utility rates, climate patterns, and even future energy price projections. This analysis extended to predicting maintenance costs by examining the age and condition of various building systems, creating a detailed timeline of expected repairs and replacements.

Market Position Optimization

Modern AI systems excel at identifying a property's optimal market position. These systems analyze vast amounts of market data to determine how different positioning strategies might affect returns. For rental properties, this might mean identifying the most profitable balance between rental rates and occupancy levels. For properties being considered for renovation, it means determining which improvements will provide the best return on investment given current and projected market conditions.

Lisa Martinez's experience with a small apartment building in Denver demonstrates this capability. The AI system analyzed current and historical rental listings in the area, examining not just pricing but also amenity packages, lease terms, and even marketing language. It identified specific amenity combinations that commanded premium rents in the local market and calculated the potential return on adding these features.

The system went further, analyzing demographic trends and consumer preference data to predict future amenity demands. It identified emerging trends in renter preferences, such as increasing demand for home office spaces and package delivery solutions, helping Lisa plan renovations that would maintain the property's competitiveness for years to come.

Risk Assessment and Mitigation

The evaluation of real estate investment risks has been transformed by AI capabilities. Modern systems conduct comprehensive risk assessments that consider multiple potential threats to investment returns. These analyses examine everything from natural disaster risks to local market volatility to potential regulatory changes.

Consider how these systems analyzed potential investments in Miami's evolving market. The AI examined flood risk using not just current FEMA maps but also climate model projections and historical storm surge data. It analyzed soil composition and groundwater levels to assess foundation risks. The system even evaluated potential insurance cost increases by analyzing claims history and regulatory trends in similar coastal markets.

The risk analysis extends to market-specific factors as well. The systems examine local employment diversity, analyzing how dependent an area's economy is on particular industries or employers. They assess the impact of potential transportation changes, considering both announced projects and historical patterns of infrastructure development. These insights help investors understand not just current risks but also how risk profiles might evolve over time.

Implementation Strategies for Success

Successfully implementing AI real estate analysis requires a thoughtful approach that combines technological capabilities with human judgment. The most successful investors have developed systematic approaches to incorporating AI insights into their decision-making processes.

David Wilson's methodology for evaluating potential investments illustrates effective implementation. He begins each analysis by clearly defining his investment criteria, helping the AI system focus on truly relevant opportunities. The system then conducts its initial analysis, but David has learned to use this as a starting point rather than a final answer.

He systematically validates AI insights through physical inspection and local market research, using the AI's analysis as a guide for what to examine most carefully. This approach helps him identify situations where local knowledge might reveal opportunities or risks that data alone couldn't capture.

The Future of AI in Real Estate

The continued evolution of AI capabilities promises to further transform real estate investing. Emerging technologies will enable even more sophisticated analysis and prediction capabilities. Virtual and augmented reality integration will transform property visualization and analysis, allowing investors to conduct detailed virtual inspections and see potential improvements overlaid on actual properties.

Machine learning systems will become increasingly sophisticated at predicting market trends and property performance. These systems will incorporate an ever-wider range of data sources, from social media sentiment to satellite imagery to Internet of Things sensor data from smart buildings.

However, the most exciting developments may come from the integration of AI with other emerging technologies. Blockchain technology could transform property transactions and record-keeping, while 3D printing and robotics could revolutionize property renovation and maintenance. AI systems will help investors understand and capitalize on these technological changes, identifying which properties are best positioned to benefit from emerging trends.

Ethical Considerations in AI Real Estate Analysis

The increasing power of AI in real estate investing raises important ethical considerations. These systems must be designed and used in ways that promote fair housing practices and avoid perpetuating historical biases in real estate markets. They should help create more equitable access to real estate investment opportunities rather than concentrating advantages among a select few.

The issue of data privacy also requires careful consideration. AI systems analyze vast amounts of personal and behavioral data to generate their insights. Ensuring this analysis respects individual privacy while maintaining analytical power represents an ongoing challenge.

Conclusion:

The Future of Real Estate Investment

As we look to the future, the role of AI in real estate investing will continue to grow and evolve. However, success will always depend on thoughtfully combining AI capabilities with human judgment and local market knowledge. The most successful investors will be those who learn to effectively leverage AI insights while maintaining a deep understanding of real estate fundamentals.

The next chapter will explore how AI can help optimize tax strategies, building on many of the analytical principles we've discussed while addressing the unique challenges of tax planning and compliance.

Chapter 10:

Ethical Considerations in AI Finance

The Human Side of Financial AI

When we talk about artificial intelligence in finance, it's easy to get caught up in the technical capabilities - the algorithms, the data processing, the prediction models. But at its heart, this technology touches something deeply personal: our relationship with money, our hopes for the future, and our sense of security. As we've explored throughout this book, AI has transformed how we manage our finances, but this transformation brings with it profound ethical questions that we must address not just as users of technology, but as human beings caring for our families and communities.

Think about your own financial journey for a moment. Every decision you make about money - whether to save or spend, invest or hold back, take a risk or play it safe - reflects your values, your dreams, and your fears. When we introduce AI into these deeply personal decisions, we're not just adding a technological tool; we're inviting an intelligent system to help shape these fundamental life choices. This reality demands that we think carefully about the ethical implications of these tools.

Privacy in the Age of Financial AI

Consider Sarah Chen's experience with her AI financial advisor. Like many of us, Sarah initially focused on the system's impressive capabilities - how it could track her spending, optimize her investments, and help plan for retirement. But one day, while reviewing her financial dashboard, she realized just how intimately this system knew her life. It knew when she visited her favorite coffee shop each morning, when she started shopping for baby supplies (before she'd told anyone about her pregnancy), and even detected the subtle changes in her spending patterns that suggested she was considering a career change.

This level of insight enables remarkably personalized financial advice, but it also raises profound questions about privacy and personal boundaries. Where do we draw the line between helpful personalization and invasive surveillance? How do we ensure that this intimate financial knowledge remains protected and isn't used in ways we never intended?

The challenge becomes even more complex when we consider how financial data interweaves with every aspect of our lives. Your spending patterns reveal your medical conditions, your political donations signal your beliefs, your shopping habits reflect your personal relationships. Modern AI systems can piece together these digital breadcrumbs to create surprisingly accurate portraits of our lives, raising important questions about data protection and personal privacy.

The Hidden Impact of Algorithmic Bias

The story of Marcus Thompson illuminates another crucial ethical challenge in AI finance. As a small business owner seeking a loan, Marcus had impeccable business credentials and strong revenue growth. Yet the AI lending systems he encountered kept offering him less favorable terms than he expected. It wasn't until he participated in a research study on algorithmic bias that he understood why: the historical data used to train these AI systems contained patterns of historical discrimination, which the algorithms had inadvertently learned to replicate.

This revelation highlights one of the most insidious challenges in AI finance: algorithmic bias often operates invisibly, making it harder to detect and correct than more overt forms of discrimination. The systems aren't programmed to discriminate - they learn to do so by analyzing historical data that reflects past societal biases. Breaking this cycle requires active intervention and constant vigilance.

The Quest for Transparency

James Wilson's experience with his AI investment advisor reveals another crucial ethical challenge in financial AI. One morning, James logged into his investment platform to find that the system had recommended selling a significant portion of his technology stocks - positions he'd held for years and felt emotionally attached to. The recommendation came with a confidence rating of 87%, but James needed more than just a number. He needed to understand the reasoning behind this potentially life-changing advice.

This scenario highlights one of the most pressing challenges in AI finance: the need for explainable artificial intelligence. It's not enough for these systems to make accurate predictions or provide optimal recommendations. They must also help users understand their reasoning in human terms. This isn't just about transparency for transparency's sake - it's about empowering people to make informed decisions about their financial futures.

The best AI systems have found creative ways to bridge this explanation gap. When Lisa Martinez's AI advisor recommended increasing her retirement contributions, it didn't just present the recommendation as a mathematical optimization. Instead, it walked her through a visual story of her financial future, showing how this change would affect her lifestyle both now and in retirement. It explained its reasoning using clear comparisons and relatable examples, helping Lisa make an informed decision about her financial future.

The Digital Divide: Ensuring Equal Access

As I've worked with different people implementing AI financial tools, I've noticed a concerning pattern emerging. While these tools have incredible potential to democratize sophisticated financial planning, they risk creating a new kind of digital divide. Some users, typically younger and more tech-savvy, quickly adapt to these tools and leverage their full capabilities. Others, often older or less comfortable with technology, struggle to access even basic features.

Consider the experience of Robert Chen, a retired teacher who initially felt overwhelmed by his AI financial planning tool. The system offered powerful capabilities for retirement planning and investment management, but its interface assumed a level of technological literacy that Robert hadn't yet developed. It wasn't until his local library offered a workshop on AI financial tools that Robert began to feel comfortable using these powerful resources.

This situation highlights a crucial ethical imperative: as we develop more sophisticated AI financial tools, we must ensure they remain accessible to everyone. This isn't just about creating user-friendly interfaces - though that's certainly important. It's about recognizing that financial empowerment through AI should be available to all, regardless of their technological expertise or educational background.

Looking Forward: The Promise and Responsibility of AI Finance

As we conclude our exploration of AI in personal finance, it's worth taking a moment to reflect on both the incredible promise and the serious responsibilities these tools bring. Throughout this book, we've journeyed through the landscape of modern financial technology, from basic budgeting tools to sophisticated market prediction systems. We've seen how AI can transform retirement planning, revolutionize real estate investment, and make sophisticated financial strategies accessible to everyone.

But we've also discovered that this power comes with significant responsibilities. As users of these tools, we must remain vigilant about data privacy, aware of potential biases, and thoughtful about how we integrate AI recommendations into our decision-making processes. We must advocate for transparency in AI systems and push for greater accessibility to ensure these powerful tools benefit everyone, not just the technologically savvy.

The future of AI in finance looks remarkably bright, but achieving its full potential requires a balanced approach. When Maria Sanchez, a young entrepreneur, first began using AI financial tools, she made a crucial observation: "These systems aren't replacing my judgment," she said, "they're enhancing it. They help me see patterns and opportunities I might miss, but the final decisions still require human wisdom and understanding."

This insight captures the essence of successful AI integration in personal finance. These tools aren't meant to replace human judgment but to augment it. They can process vast amounts of data, identify subtle patterns, and generate sophisticated recommendations. But the final decisions about our financial futures must remain firmly in human hands, guided by our values, goals, and understanding of our unique circumstances.

A Call to Thoughtful Action

As we look to the future, it's clear that AI will play an increasingly important role in personal finance. The tools will become more sophisticated, the analysis more nuanced, and the recommendations more personalized. But success in using these tools will always require maintaining a careful balance between leveraging their capabilities and exercising human judgment.

Remember Jennifer Thompson's journey with AI financial planning? When she first started using these tools, she followed their recommendations almost blindly, trusting in the technology's sophistication. But over time, she developed a more nuanced approach, learning to combine the AI's analytical insights with her own understanding of her family's needs and values. Her success came not from surrendering decision-making to the AI but from learning to use it as a powerful tool for achieving her financial goals.

This approach - thoughtful, balanced, and ethically aware - represents the future of AI in personal finance. As these tools continue to evolve, our challenge will be to harness their incredible capabilities while remaining mindful of their limitations and ethical implications. By maintaining this balance, we can work toward a future where sophisticated financial planning and investing are truly accessible to everyone, while ensuring these powerful tools serve the broader good of society.

The journey we've taken through this book is just the beginning. As AI continues to transform the financial landscape, we must remain engaged, informed, and ethically mindful users of these powerful tools. Our financial futures - and those of our communities - depend on it.

The privacy considerations in AI finance represent a particularly thorny challenge because financial data reveals so much about our lives. Every transaction tells a story – where we shop, what we value, how we spend our time. When aggregated and analyzed by AI systems, this data creates detailed portraits of our lives that go far beyond simple spending patterns.

Consider the experience of Rachel Martinez, whose AI financial advisor helped her optimize her budget and investment strategy. The system's recommendations were remarkably precise because it understood not just her spending patterns but her entire lifestyle. It knew when she typically went to the gym (from her monthly membership charges), what she liked to eat (from her grocery and restaurant purchases), and even her work schedule (from her commuting patterns). While this deep understanding enabled highly personalized financial advice, it also raised important questions about data privacy and protection.

Modern AI financial systems must balance the benefits of deep data analysis with robust privacy protections. This goes beyond simple data encryption or secure storage. These systems must consider questions like:

When does personalization cross the line into invasion of privacy? How can systems provide sophisticated analysis while minimizing the collection and storage of sensitive personal information? What happens to accumulated financial behavior data if a user decides to switch services?

The Challenge of Algorithmic Bias

The issue of algorithmic bias in financial AI systems represents one of the most significant ethical challenges in the field. These biases can manifest in subtle ways that might not be immediately apparent, even to the systems' designers. The problem becomes particularly acute in financial services because biased algorithms can perpetuate and amplify existing economic inequalities.

Take the case of mortgage lending algorithms. Traditional credit scoring systems have often disadvantaged certain demographic groups due to historical patterns of economic discrimination. When AI systems learn from this historical data, they risk perpetuating these biases in more sophisticated ways. A study by the National Bureau of Economic Research found that algorithmic lending systems, while appearing neutral, could actually charge higher interest rates to minority borrowers due to subtle patterns in the training data.

Progressive financial institutions have begun addressing these challenges through various approaches:

Diverse Training Data: Ensuring AI systems learn from diverse datasets that represent all segments of society.

Bias Testing: Implementing rigorous testing protocols to identify potential biases before systems go live.

Outcome Monitoring: Continuously analyzing system recommendations to ensure fair treatment across different demographic groups.

Transparency and Explainability

The "black box" nature of many AI systems poses particular challenges in finance, where users need to understand and trust the rationale behind important financial decisions. Modern AI financial systems must balance sophisticated analysis with clear explanations of their decision-making processes.

James Chen's experience with an AI investment advisor illustrates this challenge. The system recommended selling a long-held stock position, but James needed to understand why. The challenge for AI systems is to provide explanations that are both accurate and comprehensible to users without technical backgrounds. The best systems have developed sophisticated ways to communicate their reasoning:

Natural Language Explanations: Converting complex analytical findings into clear, conversational explanations.

Visual Decision Trees: Creating intuitive visualizations that show key factors in decisions.

Confidence Levels: Clearly communicating the certainty level of different recommendations.

The Digital Divide in Financial AI

As AI financial tools become more sophisticated, there's a risk of creating a new digital divide between those who can effectively use these tools and those who cannot. This divide could exacerbate existing economic inequalities if not carefully addressed.

- Financial institutions and AI developers have begun implementing solutions to bridge this gap:
- Educational Integration: Building learning resources directly into financial AI tools.
- Simplified Interfaces: Creating multiple levels of interaction to accommodate users with different technical capabilities.
- Community Outreach: Partnering with community organizations to provide AI financial literacy training.

The Promise and Peril of AI Finances

As we look to the future, AI financial tools will undoubtedly become even more sophisticated and capable. However, success in using these tools will always require balancing their capabilities with human judgment and ethical considerations. Here are key principles to remember:

1. AI tools are powerful aids but not infallible oracles. Always maintain healthy skepticism and cross-reference important decisions with multiple sources.

2. Privacy and security should be primary considerations when choosing AI financial tools. Research providers' data practices and security measures carefully.

3. Be aware of potential biases in AI systems and actively seek out tools that demonstrate commitment to fairness and transparency.

4. Stay informed about AI capabilities and limitations. The field evolves rapidly, and understanding these changes helps you use tools more effectively.

5. Remember that financial success requires more than just good tools – it requires discipline, patience, and clear goals.

A Pragmatic Optimism

The future of AI in personal finance is bright but requires careful navigation. These tools have democratized sophisticated financial analysis and planning, making previously exclusive capabilities available to everyone. However, this democratization comes with responsibilities:

- Users must educate themselves about both the capabilities and limitations of AI financial tools.
- Financial institutions must continue developing more transparent and ethical AI systems.
- Regulators must evolve frameworks to ensure AI financial tools serve the public good.
- Society must work to ensure equal access to these powerful financial tools.

With proper attention to these responsibilities, AI financial tools can help create a more equitable and prosperous financial future for everyone. The key is approaching these tools with informed optimism –

embracing their potential while remaining mindful of their limitations and ethical implications.

Remember, the goal isn't to replace human judgment with artificial intelligence but to enhance our decision-making capabilities with powerful analytical tools. By combining AI capabilities with human wisdom and ethical awareness, we can work toward a future where sophisticated financial planning and investing are truly accessible to all.

"Required reading for anyone serious about taking control of their finances in today's technology-driven world"

Artificial intelligence is revolutionizing personal finance, making sophisticated investment strategies accessible to everyone. This comprehensive guide transforms complex AI concepts into practical, actionable strategies that anyone can use - regardless of their technical background or financial expertise.

This isn't another investment guide - it's your comprehensive roadmap to financial success in the AI era. Whether you're saving for retirement, planning to buy a home, or simply want to make smarter financial decisions, this book will show you how to leverage AI as a powerful ally in achieving your financial goals.

Don't let the AI revolution pass you by - learn how to use these transformative tools to plan your financial future today.

ISBN 9798307922521

90000

9 798307 922521